BEGINNER TO INTERMEDIATE LEVEL

Build Business Spreadsheets
using Excel

by Kathleen Adkins

Edited by Alastair Matchett

Adkins & Matchett
NEW YORK · LONDON

Cover design and
page layout: Loraine Machlin

Illustrations: Jacque Auger

Proofreaders: Bruce Jensen
                 Joni Jensen
                 Mary Jane Kaplan
                 Karen Lynch
                 Josephine Matchett
                 Jill Stockwell
                 Norman Toy

© 1998 Adkins & Matchett Ltd

Published by Adkins & Matchett Ltd

All rights reserved. The text of this publication, or any part thereof, may not be reproduced in any manner whatsoever without written permission.

This book is intended to provide accurate information with regard to the subject matter covered. However, the author and publisher accept no responsibility for inaccuracies or omissions, and the author and publisher specifically disclaim any liability, loss, or risk, whether personal, financial, or otherwise, that is incurred as a consequence, directly or indirectly, from the use and/or application of any of the contents of this book.

Lotus is a registered trademark of Lotus Development Corporation.
Quattro Pro is a registered trademark of Novell, Inc.

Manufactured in the United States of America

ISBN 1-891112-52-X

> *To all the financial analysts I have ever taught, in appreciation of their energy, skill and concentration.*
> *– KA*

Toll-free order line: 1 (888) 414-0999

Visit us at www.adkinsmatchett.com

New York   235 Eastern Avenue, Ossining, NY 10562, 1 (914) 944-0999
London   43 Marchmont Street, London WC1N 1AP, +44-171-916-7030

ABOUT THIS BOOK

Learn to create business spreadsheets the way the pros do!

INTRODUCTION TO THE BOOK

What this book is

This book teaches you to create commonly-used business spreadsheets using Excel. It's based on years of experience teaching some of the business world's best spreadsheet users and designers: Wall Street's financial analysts.

These spreadsheet users are like racecar drivers who work hard to get the most out of their vehicle. They have to be accurate, fast and efficient. I've concentrated their best methods into this book so that you can get to be a pro Excel user as quickly as possible.

Part 1 is for beginners:
- It shows you the Excel basics;
- It warns you about common mistakes and pitfalls;
- It points out the most efficient Excel practices and shortcuts.

Part 2 is a collection of problem sets. You'll learn by creating spreadsheets that solve real-life business problems. The problems are in three sets:

    A. General business problems

    B. Financial math problems

    C. Financial projection problems

Going through the problems gives you the kind of practice you need to become a master of spreadsheet design and construction. There's no substitute for practice!

Also be sure to go through the:

Appendices
They're full of tips and commands, including some that are not discussed in detail in the problem sets.

What this workbook is not

This book is not a "feature teacher," or collection of unrelated Excel features. There are lots of Excel commands and functions you **won't** learn in this book. I want you to learn the most useful features and commands the right way. Then you'll be able to add other features and commands easily.

Good luck!

Write to me at the Adkins & Matchett website if you have comments or questions:

    kathleen@adkinsmatchett.com

Contents

Introduction 1

Part 1: Foundation skills

- A. Orientation 7
- B. Enter, delete, edit data 13
  - Test 1 21
- C. Menu commands 22
  - Test 2 28
- D. Formulas 31
  - Test 3 45
- E. The COPY command 46
  - Test 4 50
- F. Moving things around 51
  - Test 5 56
- G. Presentation 58
  - Final test, part 1 69

Part 2: Problem sets

- A. General business problems 71
  - Set 1. Simple models 77
  - Set 2. Data analysis 87
  - Set 3. Date math 95
  - Set 4. Growth calculations 103
- B. Financial math problems 111
  - Set 5. PV and FV 113
  - Set 6. NPV and IRR 121
- C. Financial projections 129
  - Set 7. Secondary calculations and plug accounts 131
  - Set 8. Financial statement projection, single sheet 139
  - Set 9. Multiple sheets 149
  - Set 10. Financial statement projection, multiple sheets 157

Appendices

- Appendix A: Efficiency 164
- Appendix B: Common business formulas and functions 167

continued on next page

Appendix C: Excel troubleshooter 171
Appendix D: Guide to formatting 173
Appendix E: Other useful commands and features 180
Appendix F: Printing 188
Appendix G: The A-B-C-D of spreadsheet design 191
Appendix H Standards and checking 193

Answers

Part 1 197
Part 2
   A. General business problems 207
   B. Financial math 215
   C. Financial projections 220

Index

Index 231

PART 1. FOUNDATION SKILLS

INTRODUCTION

INTRODUCTION

Excel

Why Excel?
Excel is only one of several good spreadsheet programs. Each one has its own strengths and problems, and all are good. This workbook features Excel instead of another product for one reason: more people and companies now use Excel than any other spreadsheet program.

If you use Lotus, Quattro Pro, or another program
Today, most modern spreadsheet programs are pretty much alike. If you use Lotus, Quattro Pro, or another program, you can still use this book to learn about good business practices in spreadsheet construction.

You'll have to find out which keystrokes or menu commands to use in place of the Excel keystrokes – a little more work for you! But the principles of good spreadsheet design still apply no matter which program you use.

Different versions of Excel
This workbook works best with these versions of Excel:

- Excel Version 5
- Excel for Windows 95
- Excel for Windows 97

What you should know before you begin

This book won't teach you how to:

- Turn on your computer
- Start Excel
- Use menus and dialog boxes
- Look through directories and drives

Sorry, you'll have to pick these skills up elsewhere. But I *will* tell you what you need to know to use Excel successfully.

© 1998 Adkins & Matchett

BUILD BUSINESS SPREADSHEETS USING EXCEL

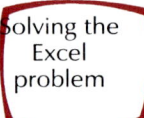
Solving the Excel problem

An Excel problem...

Excel often offers not one, not two, but three or even more ways to accomplish the same task. That's great if you like choice, but which method is best for you to use?

This book shows you the skill set you need to become an expert spreadsheet creator in Excel. I'll show you the most efficient and accurate methods, the techniques used by experts. Then I'll give you alternatives as a reference. You decide which you want to use.

Two keys to your success

Key 1: Do what the pros do
Learn the skills and methods that the experts use.

The pros spend hours each day building financial analyses with Excel. They don't waste time with anything but the most efficient and accurate methods.

Look for the Best Practices icons throughout this book. If you learn the Best Practices, you'll build a solid foundation for the more complicated spreadsheets you'll create in the future.

Practice! Practice! Practice!

Key 2: Use Excel
Turn new skills into habits by practicing them.

Using Excel skillfully is like playing a musical instrument: the key to success is to practice. In other words, try each skill or formula 3 times in a row! Return and review each of them again later.

2 Training for Finance

PART 1. FOUNDATION SKILLS

Note for experts
If you already know Excel, you can either skip this section or skim it. I recommend that you skim it. You might, just might, pick up some new tips....

> Do what the pros do – use the keyboard

KEYBOARD OR MOUSE?

Excel usually offers you two or more ways to execute the same task. For every mouse click, there's usually a keyboard command, and vice versa. Which should you use?

Use the most efficient method
I want to show you the most efficient, most accurate methods. Sometimes I'll recommend that you use the keyboard, other times the mouse. Sometimes the only way to get to a command is to use the mouse. Other times the keyboard is faster.

BEST PRACTICES

The keyboard rules!
Actually, I'm going to stress the keyboard over the mouse. Here's why:

1. **The keyboard is faster.** It eats up time to pick your hand up from the keyboard, use the mouse, put your hand back on the keyboard and continue entering data. If you want to work efficiently, learn keyboard commands.

2. **The pros use the keyboard.** Financial analysts who spend hours a day working on complex spreadsheets use keyboard commands to speed up their work.

   I know one department of a New York bank that takes away their new hires' mice for 2 months just to force them to use the keyboard!

3. **The keyboard won't stress your wrist, hand and arm** as quickly as the mouse.

When to use the mouse
Sometimes you'd be crazy to use anything but the mouse. I'll point out these situations as we come to them in this book.

If your keyboard skills are weak, or you just *love* the mouse and already have engraved some neural patterns by using it a lot, the mouse may be a better option for you. You choose!

© 1998 Adkins & Matchett

BUILD BUSINESS SPREADSHEETS USING EXCEL

FOUNDATION SKILLS – YOU HAVE TO HAVE 'EM

You need to have some basic skills before you move to Part 2, the main part of this book. The skills listed below are foundation skills which you will use again and again. They must become so much a part of you that you don't have to think about them.

For example, if you're in a bicycle race, you should not be thinking about how to ride the bicycle. You should simply be riding – shifting, braking, turning – while you think about your race strategy.

Same thing with spreadsheet construction. You shouldn't have to stop and think about how to copy a formula. You should be able to copy it without thinking about the process of copying. You need to save your thinking for more important subjects, like how to structure your spreadsheet and find the most effective solution to a problem.

Checklist of skills

These are the basic skills you need to master in Part 1:

- **Understand the Excel layout**
- **Enter data**
- **Edit data**
- **Create simple formulas**
- **Copy data and formulas**
- **Use SUM to add numbers**
- **Format text**
- **Widen columns**
- **Print**
- **Save**

More later

As you go through Part 1, you may find yourself wondering about some feature that hasn't been covered yet. Remember that Part 1 is an introduction. You'll probably find out more about the feature in Part 2, when you've got the background to appreciate it.

How to put these skills in the bank – your knowledge bank

Do it now!

As I said above, you have to practice these skills. So try everything in this section several times. Look for the **Do it now** icons.

Just as a guitar player doesn't have time to think about how to finger a D chord during a performance, you can't afford to be wondering if that Cut command really worked while you're puzzling your way through an important financial forecast.

OK, let's get started!

4 Training for Finance

Part One:

Foundation Skills

© 1998 Adkins & Matchett

PART 1. FOUNDATION SKILLS

A. ORIENTATION

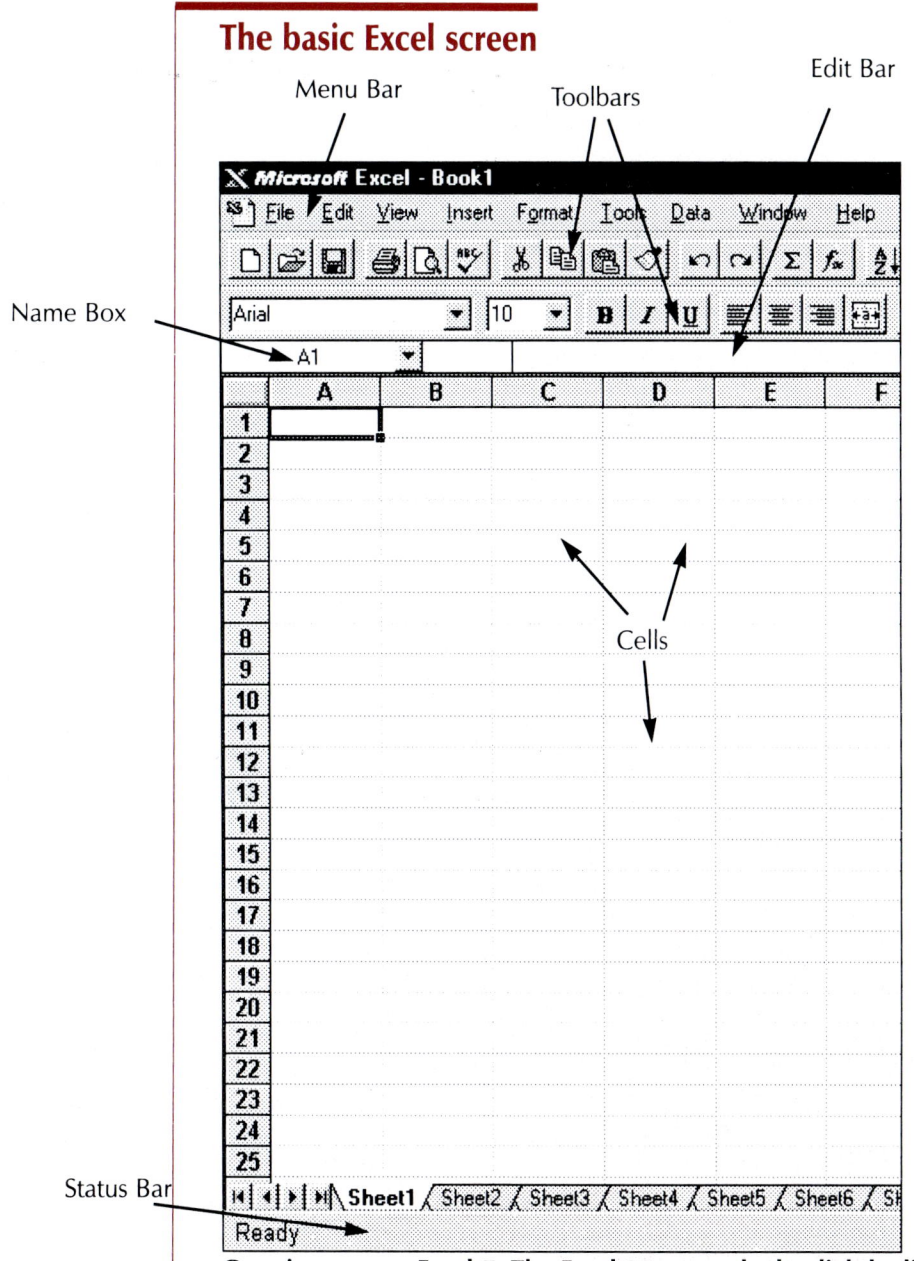

Opening screen, Excel 7. The Excel 97 screen looks slightly different.

The *pointer* (sometimes called cursor) shows you where you are. Notice the pointer (which looks like a box) is in Cell A1, and the Name Box also says A1.

© 1998 Adkins & Matchett

BUILD BUSINESS SPREADSHEETS USING EXCEL

2. The cell: basic Excel building block

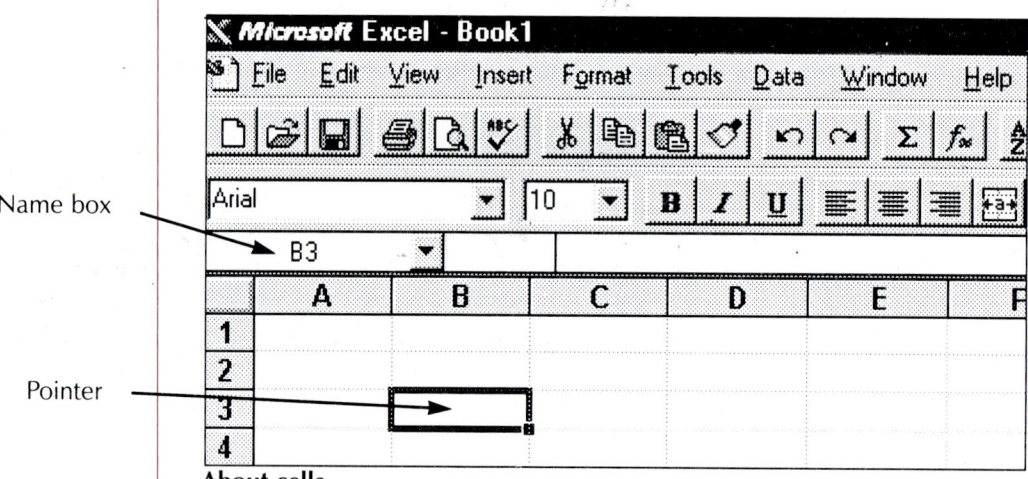

Name box
Pointer

About cells

- **Cells can hold numbers, words, or formulas.**

- **Every cell has an address.**
  Sample: Look at the illustration above. The pointer is sitting on Cell B3.
  How can you tell?
  Look at the Column heading (B) and the Row number (3).
  Look at the Name box. It shows you the pointer's address (B3).

- **The column address always goes first (B3, not 3B).**

Training for Finance

PART P. FOUNDATION SKILLS

EXERCISE 1 ▶
Addresses

PAPER & PENCIL EXERCISE

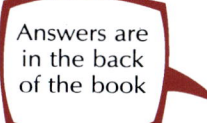
Answers are in the back of the book

Exercise 1. What are the cell addresses?

Identify cells in this diagram.

Label each shaded cell with its Excel address.

	A	B	C
1			
2			
3			
4			
5			
6			
7			
8			

© 1998 Adkins & Matchett   9

BUILD BUSINESS SPREADSHEETS USING EXCEL

ORIENTATION

OK, let's go to the spreadsheet.

Start Excel. You'll see a blank spreadsheet on the screen.

Find the:
- Toolbars. Does your screen show one toolbar or more than one?
- Menu bar
- Edit bar
- Name box
- Status Bar. Does it say READY? If it doesn't, press the **Esc** key a few times.
- Pointer

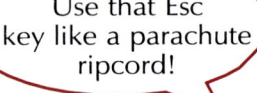

Use that Esc key like a parachute ripcord!

Make sure you can find these items on your keyboard:
- Number pad
- Two Enter keys (one on the Number pad, one on the regular keyboard)
- Esc (Escape) key

About the Escape key

The Escape key is your escape hatch. When something bad happens or the cursor won't move, try hitting Escape first. It can't hurt, and it might help.

Do it now!

Navigation

Move the cursor around.

1. Click in different cells with the mouse.

2. Try moving the pointer with these keys:

3. Try these keys. How do they affect the pointer? Experiment and find out for yourself.

10 Training for Finance

PART 1. FOUNDATION SKILLS

Do it now!

More power to you

Move to Cell B4.

Now hold down **CTRL** and press **Home**.

CTRL Home always takes you "**home**" – to the upper left corner.

Use your mouse to click on a cell away from the upper left corner, then press **CTRL Home**.

Now try **CTRL** and press the **DOWN ARROW** key.

The POWER of CTRL

Where are you?

You've hit the bottom of the spreadsheet. The pointer "flew" until it couldn't go any further.

Notice how many rows you have to work with!

Fly back

Fly home with **CTRL Home**.

KEY KNOWLEDGE

CTRL-ARROW KEY makes the pointer "fly" until it hits something - in this case, the end of the spreadsheet.

Column labels and how to read them

Fly to the right with **CTRL-RIGHT ARROW**.

You've hit the right side of the spreadsheet. What does IV mean?

Excel labels its columns A - Z. After A, it move to AA - AZ, BA - BZ, and so on until it reaches Column Number 256, which is Column IV.

The worksheet

How big is this thing?

- **No. of Rows = 16,384** *(pre-Excel 97)*   **65,536** *(Excel 97)*
- **No. of Columns = 256**

© 1998 Adkins & Matchett   **11**

BUILD BUSINESS SPREADSHEETS USING EXCEL

Multiple sheets

Look at the sheet tabs at the bottom of the screen.

Notice the white sheet tab

The sheet tabs

The white tab is the sheet you're on. Use your mouse to click on another sheet table.

When you're through, click back to Sheet1.

You can see that you have a number of different worksheets collected into a workbook. At the end of Part 2, you'll start to use more than one worksheet in your spreadsheets. For now, you'll work only on one sheet.

I've told you about these multiple worksheets now just so you will know what has happened if you click on one by accident.

PART 1. FOUNDATION SKILLS

B. ENTER, DELETE, EDIT DATA

The most basic Excel skill is entering information into cells.

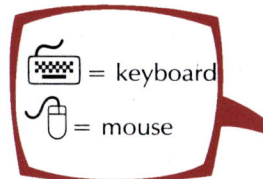

ENTER DATA STEP BY STEP

How to put entries in cells.

1. Move to the cell you want to use.

2. Type the entry you want to make, then:

3. Press **ENTER** or an **ARROW KEY**

    Click in any cell, or click the green check mark that appears in the Edit bar when you're entering data.

   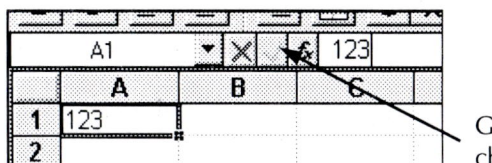
   Green check mark

About that green check mark

You'll only see the green check mark when you are actually entering something in a cell. Normally you don't see either the green check mark or the red X. The red X? It works like the **Esc** key. See the next page.

Do it now!

Input data

Input this data. (Skip Row 1 for now.)

	A	B
1		
2	Sales	500
3	Expenses	325
4	Margin	175
5	Taxes	75
6	Profit	100

Excel automatically aligns your work

Notice two things:

- **Words**   Labels align left.
- **Numbers**   Values align right.

You can change these alignments if you want. Leave them as is for now.

© 1998 Adkins & Matchett   **13**

BUILD BUSINESS SPREADSHEETS USING EXCEL

> **DELETE AN ENTRY**
>
> What if you want to erase a cell's contents?
>
> Press the **Delete** key. (*Don't* use the **Backspace** key!)
>
> (There's a way to delete with the mouse, but it's somewhat confusing. Stick with the Delete key for now.)

Correcting your mistakes

What if you make a mistake?

You'll make mistakes and change your mind during data entry – yes, even you.

You can fix your mistakes a number of ways.

Do it now!

Delete data

Add new entries in Row 7.

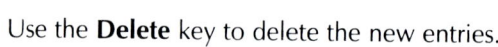

5	Taxes	75
6	Profit	100
7	Dividends	25

Use the **Delete** key to delete the new entries.

Don't click in the cell, then backspace over each character! Just hit **Delete**! Backspacing is a big waste of time!

No – NO – NO!

Type over the bad entry

You can simply type over the entry.

Change the **Sales** figure to 550 by typing over it.
Change the **Margin** figure to 225 by typing over it.

KEY KNOWLEDGE

It's a waste of time to delete an entry before you type over it.

"Throw away" an entry before you enter it

Can you "throw away" an entry before you complete it? Yes!

  Press **ESC** instead of **ENTER**.

  Click the red X on the Edit Bar.

Do it now!

Try it both ways several times.
   Go to Row 7 and type something, then cancel the entry before pressing Enter. Do it several times. Try both methods, the keyboard and the mouse.

14 Training for Finance

PART 1. FOUNDATION SKILLS

BEST PRACTICES

THE STATUS BAR AND THE EDIT BAR

Learn to read the Status Bar and Edit Bar. These two features contain valuable information that can help you figure out problems and mistakes.

The more sophisticated your work, the more you'll rely on these features.

Move to A1 and prepare to enter the label P&L in the cell.

Before you make the entry, look at the Status Bar at the bottom of the screen.
- **It should say Ready.**

Look at the Edit Bar. It's right under the menu and toolbar area at the top of the screen.
- **It should be empty.**
- **You will not see the green checkmark or the red X.**

The Edit Bar	The Status Bar

Before you start to enter data

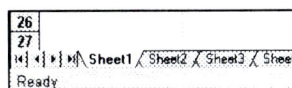

The pros keep their eye on the Status Bar and Edit Bar!

Type the letter P, the first letter of your entry. Now look at the Status Bar and the Edit Bar.

The Edit Bar	The Status Bar

After you begin to enter data

The Edit Bar	Shows that you're entering data. Look for the first letter of your entry and the green and red icon buttons.
The Status Bar	It will say Enter, not Ready, when you're in the middle of an entry. (It's telling you what to do to complete the entry: "Press Enter.")

Keep your eye on the Edit and Status Bars

Try entering and cancelling entries while you keep an eye on the Edit and Status Bars.

© 1998 Adkins & Matchett

BUILD BUSINESS SPREADSHEETS USING EXCEL

No – NO – **NO!**

NEVER, NEVER

Never "erase" a cell by hitting the **spacebar**. You have not erased the cell — you've simply replaced its contents with a space.

This practice will cause untold trouble in a sophisticated spreadsheet and is the sure mark of an amateur. Even worse, spaces are not visible and are hard to find.

Just don't do it!

Summary: What if you make a mistake?

KEY KNOWLEDGE

Excel "remembers" any special format applied to a cell and continues to apply it even if you type something new.

- If the entry is short and simple: Just type over it.
- If you want to get rid of the entry: Press the **Delete** key.
- If you change your mind while typing: Press **Esc**.

BASIC NUMBER FORMATTING

This section is just an introduction to formatting. Once you finish Part 1, you can find out more about formatting in Appendix D.

Do it now!

Automatic number formatting

You can change the appearance of numbers as you enter them. One way to control formatting is by typing the format as you input the number.

Move to an empty cell. Enter $400.
Move to another cell and enter 2,300.
Move to a third cell. Enter 10%.

What happens if you change the contents of these cells?

Delete $400 and enter 20 in the same cell. The number shows up as $20.

Experiment with these different formats and see what happens if you type new numbers into formatted cells.

Do it now!

Negative numbers

What about negatives?

Type –300 into an unused cell. You should see **–300** appear in the cell.

Below this cell, type –$300. You should see **($300)** in the cell.

Negative numbers appear in (**parentheses**) whenever you type a dollar sign with your numbers.

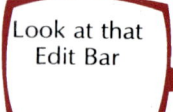

Look at that Edit Bar

16 Training for Finance

PART 1. FOUNDATION SKILLS

CELL WIDTH: HOW WIDE IS THAT CELL, REALLY?

What if you type a word or phrase that's longer than the cell is wide?

Try it and see what happens.

Do it now!

Enter a long phrase

Delete anything you have entered in A1, B1, and C1 and place your pointer on A1.

Enter the phrase *Profit and loss statement*.

What happens to the cell?

	A	B	C
1	Profit and loss statement		
2	Sales	500	
3	Expenses	325	

Does the phrase actually appear in B1 and C1? How can you tell?

Hint Put the pointer on A1 and look in the Edit Bar. Now put the pointer on B1 and look in the Edit Bar.

You'll see that there is nothing in Cells B1 and C1, even though the phrase looks like it has "run over" into those cells when you look at the spreadsheet.

Now enter something in Cell B1.

KEY KNOWLEDGE

A cell can hold up to 256 characters

	A	B	C
1	Profit and	Yeasstatement	
2	Sales	500	
3	Expenses	325	

What happened to the text in A1? Remember to check the Edit Bar.

Delete the contents of Cell B1 and watch what happens to the text.

Summary

- An entry wider than the cell will show up on the screen if the next cell(s) are empty, but the entry itself always occupies only one cell.
- If you enter something in the cell to the right, you won't be able to read the spillover any longer.

© 1998 Adkins & Matchett   **17**

BUILD BUSINESS SPREADSHEETS USING EXCEL

Long entries

What should you do about long entries? You have two choices:

- **PRO:** Widen the column.
- **AMATEUR:** Skip empty columns to the right of the entry.

Of course you know I want you to widen the column.

WIDEN A COLUMN

You can adjust the column width several different ways with the mouse. Make sure you are not editing a cell.

1. Put the **mouse pointer on the line between columns** in the column letter row at the top of the spreadsheet. When you're over the boundary, the pointer will change shape to look like this:

   When you see the pointer change its shape, **click, hold, and drag** the column boundary to the size you want.

2. Or double-click the boundary and Excel will automatically fit the column to its widest entry.

KEY KNOWLEDGE
The width of the entire column changes. You can't create different widths within the same column.

Do it now. Widen Column A to fit the text it contains.

EDITING YOUR INPUTS

Sometimes it's easier just to type over a cell with new content, but sometimes it's easier to edit the cell and just change one letter or word.

Do it now!

Edit your data

Prepare to change *Profit and loss statement* to *Profit & loss statement*.

1. Go to A1.

2.  Press **F2**.

    Click in the Edit Bar. (Work in the Edit Bar, not in the cell. Later you'll disable the cell editing to get to another feature which allows you to proofread formulas easily.)

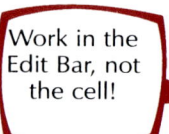
Work in the Edit Bar, not the cell!

3. Use the **Arrow keys** or **CTRL Left arrow** to move to *and*.

4. Use **Backspace** or **Delete** to erase and type &

5.  Press **Enter**   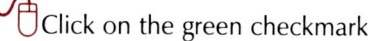 Click on the green checkmark.

18 Training for Finance

PART 1. FOUNDATION SKILLS

EDIT A CELL

Put the pointer on the cell you want to edit.

1. Go into Edit mode.

    Press **F2**

    Double-click the cell (NOT the method you will use in this book!)

   or

   Click on the Edit Bar

2. Move to the data you want to change and delete it or add to it.

    Use **Arrow keys** to move to the element you want to change. Use **Backspace** or **Delete** if necessary.

    Select the element you want to change.

3. Enter the change.

Do it now!

Do it now! Edit your work

1. Delete the word *Statement* from Cell A1.
2. Change *Taxes* to *Tax*.
3. Change *Year 1* to *1st Year*.

EXERCISE 2 ▶
Data in cells

PAPER & PENCIL EXERCISE

Exercise 2: Lock your data up in cells

1. Look at the example below. Which cell is the active cell (the cell the pointer is on)?

	A	B	C
1	Profit and	Year 1	
2	Sales	500	
3	Expenses	325	

   (B2 — 500)

   Cell address of the pointer: _____

2. Is the active cell being edited?

   ☐ Yes   ☐ No

3. How can you tell?

   _____

© 1998 Adkins & Matchett   **19**

BUILD BUSINESS SPREADSHEETS USING EXCEL

EXERCISE 3 ▶
Set up a spreadsheet

Exercise 3. Set up a small spreadsheet

In this exercise, you'll use everything you've learned so far to set up a small spreadsheet. You'll:

- Enter words and numbers
- Widen a column
- Edit a word
- Edit a number

Click on another sheet tab (at the bottom of the spreadsheet). Do this exercise on another sheet. To get to the other sheet, click on its tab.

1. Enter manufacturing expenses for two quarters.

Mfg. Expenses	Qtr 1	Qtr 2
Labor	8000	8025
Supplies	6000	6500
Electricity	200	240
Tool and die	750	750
Robotics	1000	1050
Depreciation	500	500

2. Make these changes:

   i. Change "Mfg." To Manufacturing
   ii. Change Supplies to Materials
   iii. Change Labor to Labor costs
   iv. Change Qtr 1's labor costs to 8125

3. Adjust column widths appropriately.

Leave the spreadsheet on the screen. You'll save it in the next section.

20 Training for Finance

PART 1. FOUNDATION SKILLS

PAPER & PENCIL EXERCISE

Test #1

How much do you know?

1. Look at the example below. Is the active cell being edited?

   ❏ Yes   ❏ No

   How can you tell?

   _____

2. Which method(s) should you use to delete a cell's contents?
   ❏ spacebar   ❏ Delete key   ❏ Backspace key

3. What does the following Status Bar message mean?

   Ready _____

4. You can widen part of a column.
   ❏ True   ❏ False

5. If you have to make a very long entry, you should:
   ❏ Widen the column   ❏ Skip several columns to give the entry room

Answers are in the back of the book.

© 1998 Adkins & Matchett **21**

BUILD BUSINESS SPREADSHEETS USING EXCEL

C. MENU COMMANDS

About the menus

You will need to use the menus to perform many tasks when you build a spreadsheet. The menu contains almost all the commands you can ever use in Excel.

Look at the menu bar. Each word on the menu bar opens a menu of related commands. For instance, the File menu contains commands for opening, closing and saving files and for general functions that apply to an entire file. The Edit menu houses commands that let you change data already in your spreadsheet.

Menus vs. Icons

Many of the menu commands are also available by clicking icons. If you like to use the mouse, you can find icons on different toolbars that will let you use your mouse more frequently.

You can even customize your toolbars to contain your favorite icons – I'll show you how later. But for now, as you're learning, **use the menu to issue most commands**. You'll get familiar with Excel's set of commands more quickly.

HOW TO

OPEN A MENU

You can open a menu several different ways:

1.   Press **ALT**, then release
   ARROW to the menu you want to open
   Press **ENTER**

2.   Click on the menu

3.   Press **ALT**, then release
   Type the underscored letter of the menu you want to open

Note: Although this method may seem slow now because you have to stop and look at the underscored letters, it's definitely **the fastest, most efficient way to enter commands** once you are more used to Excel. You will find that your fingers remember a command after you've used it several times. If you're a good typist, this method is by far the fastest. Fingers can move faster than hands!

BEST PRACTICES

22 Training for Finance

PART 1. FOUNDATION SKILLS

Read this, don't do it! It's a comparison of two different methods for using menus!

Keyboard vs. Mouse for the command to close a file

 Use your fingers
Tap **ALT** and release
Type **f c**

 Use your hand
Move your hand from the keyboard to the mouse
Move the mouse to the **File** menu
Click
Move to the **Close** command
Click
Move your hand back to the keyboard

GET OUT OF A MENU

To back out of a menu and return to the spreadsheet:

 Press **ESC**. You may need to press **ESC** repeatedly until you return to the SST

 Click in the spreadsheet

Do it now!

Build your skills

Open the **EDIT** menu and look at the commands without selecting any of them.

Then open other menus and examine them.

Try all the different ways to open menus. Use the keyboard method unless you're really, really uncomfortable with it.

Back out of each menu without using any commands.

Do it now!

Grayed commands

Some commands are available only under certain special conditions.

Open the **Edit** menu. Notice the **Links** and **Object** commands are grayed – you can't use them under normal conditions.

If a command is grayed, you can't use it. These commands become available only under special circumstances.

Ghost menus...

© 1998 Adkins & Matchett **23**

BUILD BUSINESS SPREADSHEETS USING EXCEL

Do it now!

Submenus

Any menu command with an arrowhead to its right contains a submenu.

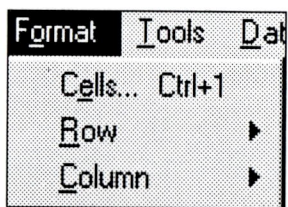

Arrowheads mark submenus

Go to the **Format** menu. Notice that the **Row** command has an arrowhead.

Go to the **Row** command and look at the submenu that opens up.

Escape from the submenu by pressing **Esc**.

Do it now!

Dialog boxes

Menu commands that end in . . . lead to dialog boxes.

These little boxes offer you more choices or ask you a question.

Go to the **Edit** menu and open the **Delete . . .** command.

Escape from a dialog box by pressing **Esc** or clicking **Cancel**.

Explore! Find out for yourself

Explore the menus without actually issuing any commands. Remember that you can always escape from any command that has an arrowhead or ends in . . .

Do it now! Save

The first time you save a file

Right now, you should have the Manufacturing costs spreadsheet on your screen. If you don't, go back to Exercise 3 and create it now.

It's time to save your file. Use the menu command to save.

Look at the name bar at the top of the screen. Even though you haven't saved your file yet, it has a default name: **Book1**. *The word "book" refers to "workbook," Excel's name for the multiple-sheet file you're working on now.*

The first time you save a file, you can give it your own descriptive name and select its address.

24 Training for Finance

PART 1. FOUNDATION SKILLS

Do it now!
File Save
ALT f s

Open the File menu

Select **Save**.

Name the file **COSTS**.   (*I've typed the name in capital letters, but you don't have to! Use lower case; it's easier.*)

    ALT f s COSTS   ENTER

Yes	**COSTS**	
No	**COSTS.**	The period prevents Excel from adding the XLS extension, making your file hard to find later.
No	**COSTS.XLS**	Too much work – Excel will add the extension for you.

Notice the name bar at the top of the screen. It should now say **COSTS.XLS**.

Do it now!

Later saves

After you have saved a file, the **Save** command works differently. It saves the new copy over the old one, automatically updating your file copy.

Try it now.   **ALT f s**

It works so quickly that you probably won't even notice the save happening.

Do it now!
File Save As
ALT f a

Saving your work

Never trust in one file! Always make extra copies of important files for your own safety. To make a spare copy, use the **Save As** command.

Do it now:

    File

    Save As

Type a new name, like **COSTS1**

Complete the operation by **Enter**ing or clicking **OK**.

Do it now!
File Close
ALT f c

Close a file

Now close the file.

    File Close

© 1998 Adkins & Matchett

BUILD BUSINESS SPREADSHEETS USING EXCEL

Do it now!

File Open
ALT f o

Open a file

Use **File Open** to open up **COSTS**.

You could type the name **COSTS** in the file name box, but it's easier to pick the name off the list of files.

 Use **Tab** or **Shift Tab** to get to the **File name** box.
Type the first letter of the file you want.

If several files begin with that letter, keep typing the letter until you reach your file. Or use the arrow keys to move the cursor.

Press **ENTER**.

 Click on the name of the file you want.

More about closing and saving files

Excel does not automatically save your changes when you close a file.

Change a cell in COSTS. Then close the file.

Notice the different response: now Excel asks you if you want to save your changes. You must decide to either keep the changes or throw them away by closing without saving.

This feature protects you from yourself. If you make a terrible mistake in a spreadsheet (and everyone does, sooner or later), sometimes the easiest thing to do is to close the file without saving it and reopen the old, clean version. Saving your file under a different name keeps a historical record of your previous work. Another good way to recover from mistakes!

WARNING

Do it now!

Which choice is pre-selected? If you press **ENTER**, will Excel save the changes or throw them away?

BEST PRACTICES

Shortcut to opening your files

Excel has a great shortcut for opening your files.

Open the **FILE** command and look at the bottom part of the menu. It should contain a list of the files you've used most recently.

Your list should read:

<u>1</u>: COSTS1.XLS
<u>2</u>: COSTS.XLS

Notice the <u>underscored</u> numbers in the list of recently used files. You can open one of these files by typing its number.

26 Training for Finance

PART 1. FOUNDATION SKILLS

Do it now!
**File Open
ALT f 2**

Shortcut

Open COSTS now, using the shortcut.

ALT f 2

New file

Do it now!
**File New
ALT f n**

Suppose you want to start a new file.

Use **File New** to bring up a fresh spreadsheet. You can choose different templates, or preset spreadsheet forms, at this point. Use the generic **Workbook** form if you're offered a choice.

Do it now.

What is the name of the new file?

Back to COSTS

Close the new file. You should see COSTS on the screen.

**EXERCISE 4 ▶
Getting around**

**PAPER & PENCIL
EXERCISE**

Exercise 3: Getting around the menus

1. Which key do you press to get to the menu bar?

2. The Edit menu has a command called Clear. What can it erase?

3. How do you "throw away" an entry before you enter it?

4. Which menu has commands that change the size of your view?
   Hint: explore the menus on your own to discover the answer.

5. Which menu has a command to delete a worksheet?

© 1998 Adkins & Matchett

BUILD BUSINESS SPREADSHEETS USING EXCEL

PAPER & PENCIL

Test #2

How much do you know?

1. Does Excel automatically save your changes when you close a file?
   ☐ Yes ☐ No

2. Which command do you use if you want to save an extra copy of your file?

3. You've just made a horrible error that would take a long time to fix. What could you do to recover?

4. Look at the **Window** menu on your screen now. If you wanted to, could you **Unhide** a window now?
   ☐ Yes ☐ No

5. How do you know?

6. You should always type the full filename when you save (COSTS.XLS)
   ☐ Yes ☐ No

7. Which key:

   Puts you on the menu bar?

   Lets you back out of a menu without activating any of its commands?

Answers are in the back of the book.

Training for Finance

PART 1. FOUNDATION SKILLS

UNDOING MISTAKES

The Undo / Redo command

You're now going to learn a command that will be your constant companion for as long as you use Excel. It's the lifesaver command, the "Ooops!" command, the magic "rewind" button that lets you recover from your own mistakes — as long as you catch them in time. And you can even repeat the command to undo the undo!

Limits

The Undo command is great, but it undoes only the last command you issued. It also doesn't work on some settings changes.

> The lifesaver! Learn this one!

BEST PRACTICES

The Undo shortcut

Open the **Edit** menu and find the **Undo** command at the top of the list. Notice the letters at the right?

Excel has special shortcut keys for commands that you'll use frequently.

CTRL Z is the keyboard shortcut for the Undo command. There are some mouse shortcuts you can find on your own later. The keyboard command is quick and handy; give it a try.

© 1998 Adkins & Matchett

BUILD BUSINESS SPREADSHEETS USING EXCEL

Do it now!

CTRL Z

Undo it!

Type your name in any cell.

Hold down **CTRL** and press **Z**.

Now do it again. What happens?

Do another **CTRL Z**.

Play around with this feature until you're comfortable with it.

Try to give the **Undo** command with one hand.

Use your little finger, left hand, to hold down the **CTRL** key.

Tap **Z** with another finger.

Ready for formulas

Now that you know how to enter and edit data, issue menu commands, and use keyboard shortcuts like CTRL Z, you're ready for the real stuff: *formulas*.

D. Formulas

Formulas are a spreadsheet's engine — its most important part!

Understand formulas
Mental prep

When you write formulas in Excel, you'll need to use operation signs and follow order of operation rules. Here's a quick overview:

Operations	Operation signs in Excel	
Addition	+	
Subtraction	-	
Multiplication	*	
Division	/	
Exponentiation	^	*SHIFT 6 on keyboard*

More complicated operations, like finding square roots, often require the use of a function. You'll learn more about functions later.

Order of operations
Look at this problem:

$$x = 2 + 3 * 5$$

Is the solution 25 or 17?

The math rules for order of operations determine that the answer is 17. You must multiply before you add.

Quick review of order of operation rules
1. Operations inside parentheses are performed first.
2. Multiplication and division are performed before addition and subtraction.

Formulas in Excel
Writing formulas in Excel is almost like writing regular algebraic formulas. But there are *a few differences*:

1. **Write only the right side of the formula.**
   Algebra formula: $x = (3+7)/5$

   Excel formula: $=(3+7)/5$

Start with =

2. **Always start formulas with =.**
   The equal sign says "Compute this" to Excel. If you don't use it, Excel won't calculate the formula.

   $= 1 + 2$

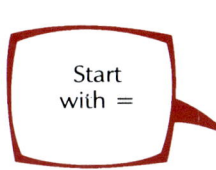

© 1998 Adkins & Matchett

BUILD BUSINESS SPREADSHEETS USING EXCEL

3. Don't use spaces in formulas!
In some cases, Excel could get confused, and that's the last thing you want.

Yes: =4/(3-1)

No: =4 / (3- 1)

4. Always use multiplication signs!
Excel doesn't recognize the algebraic convention of leaving out the multiplication sign.

Yes: =4*(2+3)   You must use the multiplication sign.

No: =4(2+3)   Excel will not understand this construction. If you use it, you'll get an error message.

EXERCISE 5 ▶ Formula logic

PAPER & PENCIL EXERCISE

Exercise 5: Formula logic

Three of these formulas won't work in Excel. Find them and describe what's wrong with them.

1. =(4+3)(5-2)

2. =4+3

3. =12^2

4. 15/3

5. =7(3-1)

OK, now you're ready to learn the key to writing useful business formulas..

The key to useful formulas in business spreadsheets

Always use cell references in your formulas.

In a real spreadsheet, you would almost never write a formula like =4+3. You'd use cell references.

Suppose you need to create a formula that subtracts expenses from sales to get gross margin.

	A	B
1	Sales	140
2	Expenses	100
3	Gross margin	

Sales - Expenses

What's the formula to calculate gross margin?

NO =140-100   **YES** =B1-B2

KEY KNOWLEDGE
Use cell references, not raw numbers, in your formulas

32 Training for Finance

PART 1. FOUNDATION SKILLS

Why do good formulas use cell references?

Because you can change the data in the cells that the formula references, and the formula will recalculate itself automatically. All good business spreadsheets rely on this capability. If you didn't need it, you could just use a hand calculator to get your answers.

You'll see much more about the value of this feature as you go through Part 2.

I know you'd like to go right to Excel, but if you haven't used a spreadsheet before, you should get comfortable with formulas before you start using the keyboard and mouse. Remember, your spreadsheet is only as good as its formulas. They have to be right.

Cell references — the difference between amateurs and professionals!

EXERCISE 6 ▶ Write formulas

PAPER & PENCIL EXERCISE

Exercise 6: Write formulas

A. Write formulas to fill in the large boxed cells. Use cell references! You should be able to write the formulas without referring to a spreadsheet.

	A	B	
1	Sales	400	
2	COGS as % of Sales	75%	
3	COGS		*Sales * COGS as % of sales*
4			
5	Cash	23	
6	Accounts receivable	42	
7	Inventory	12	
8	Total current assets		*Add*
9			
10	Net income	64	
11	Number of shares	150	
12	Earnings per share		*Divide No. of shares into Net income*
13			
14	Fixed assets	250	
15	Depreciation	140	
16	Net fixed assets		*Subtract Depn from Fixed assets*

© 1998 Adkins & Matchett

BUILD BUSINESS SPREADSHEETS USING EXCEL

Exercise 6: Write formulas, *continued*

B. **Look at the numbers below. Use their cell addresses to write the following formulas:**

HINT: Pay attention to order of operations! Use parentheses if necessary.

	A	B	C	D
1				
2		14		
3	2			
4				6
5		3		
6			11	
7				
8			4	

a. _____ Raise 14 – 2 to the 11th power.

b. _____ Subtract 2 from 3 and multiply by 4.

c. _____ Multiply 3 times 4 times 6 and divide the result by 2.

d. _____ Add 6 to 3 times 11.

Do it now!

Write formulas!

OK, let's go to Excel.

Excel formula keys Find these keys:

+   -   /   *   ^   (   )   =

BEST PRACTICES

Notice that you have two sets of most of these keys. *Use the set of operation signs on the number pad* — you don't have to hold down the **SHIFT** key to get **+** and *****

Notice that you can use the number pad's **Enter** key at any time.

If your number pad doesn't work, try pressing your *Num Lock* key. Look for it above the number pad.

FIND OUT FOR YOURSELF

Notice the extra **Enter** key on the number pad. Does it operate just like the other **Enter** key? Try it out and see for yourself.

34 Training for Finance

PART 1. FOUNDATION SKILLS

Do it now!

Write your first formulas

Open a new spreadsheet and set up these cells:

	A	B
1	Formula practice 1	
2		
3	Sales	140
4	Expenses	100
5	Gross margin	*Sales - Expenses*

Widen Column A .

To arrive at the gross margin, you have to subtract expenses from sales. Your first formula will be a subtraction formula.

HOW TO

ENTER A FORMULA

1.	Move to the formula cell.	Move to **B5**.
2.	Start the formula.	Type =
3.	Select the first input cell.	Click on **B3**.
4.	Type the operation sign.	Type the subtraction sign -
5.	Select the next input cell.	Click on **B4**.
6.	Enter the formula.	Press **ENTER**.
		Answer: **40**

That's it! Now look at the formula cell B5. You should see the result, 40.

Leave the pointer on **B5** and look at the **Edit Bar**. You'll see the formula in the **Edit Bar**:   =B3 – B4

Put the Edit Bar to work

BEST PRACTICES

Inputs and outputs

It's useful to think of inputs and outputs when you write formulas.

In the example, *Sales* and *Expenses* are **inputs**. They feed into the formula. *Gross margin* is an **output**. It's the result of a formula based on the inputs.

© 1998 Adkins & Matchett

BUILD BUSINESS SPREADSHEETS USING EXCEL

KEY KNOWLEDGE

Once you have created a formula, you can change its input cells as much as you like and the formula will change its results to match.

Formula power

Remember when I told you that using cell references gave formulas their power? Now it's time to see that power for yourself.

Move to B3 and change the sales figure to 150.

What happens to the formula cell?
Play around with the two input cells B3 and B4 and watch what happens to the formula.

What happens if Expenses are bigger than Sales?

Change Sales back to 140 and Expenses back to 100.

Formula input tips

1. If the input cells are close to the formula cell, as they are in this exercise, you may want to use the keyboard method. But in most cases, the mouse is your best choice for formula construction.

2. You can enter data by clicking on a different cell with the mouse. Formulas are different. If you click on a cell, you place that cell reference in the formula.

   To enter a formula

   Press **ENTER**.

   Click the green check mark on the Edit Bar.

3. There's one method of formula construction I recommend you ***do not use***.

   Don't type the input cell addresses. Typing the addresses works, but it's painfully slow, particularly when you're constructing complex formulas based on cells that are distant from the formula cell. And you're more likely to make mistakes.

WARNING

Do it now!

Continue your formula practice

Add some new inputs to your work. *(This example begins on Page 35.)*

	A	B
1	Formula practice 1	
2		
3	Sales	140
4	Expenses	100
5	Gross margin	40	= B3 - B4
6		
7	Selling expenses	10
8	Supplies	5
9	Overhead	8
10	Total operating expenses		*Selling exp. + Supplies + Overhead*

36 Training for Finance

PART 1. FOUNDATION SKILLS

Add up operating expenses

Build the formula for operating expenses. You're going to add the three cells in B7, B8, and B9.

This formula adds three cells instead of subtracting one from another, but its construction principles are the same.

1. Move to the formula cell.   Move to B10.
2. Start the formula.   Type =
3. Select the first input cell.   Click on B7.
4. Type the operation sign.   Type the addition sign +
5. Select the next input cell.   Click on B8.
6. Type the operation sign.   Type the addition sign +
7. Select the next input cell.   Click on B9.
6. Enter the formula.   **Enter**

   Answer: **23**

Here's where the mouse becomes useful! Use it to build formulas!

Do it now!

Practice 1, continued

Continue to build formulas. Add these inputs:

	A	B	
1	Formula practice 1		
2			
3	Sales	140	
4	Expenses	100	
5	Gross margin	40	= B3 - B4
6			
7	Selling expenses	10	
8	Supplies	5	
9	Overhead	8	
10	Total operating expenses	23	= B7 + B8 + B9
11			
12	Operating margin	17	*Gross margin - operating expenses*
13	Non-operating expenses	14	
14	Net income	3	*Operating margin - non-op. expenses*

You can try these formulas on your own if you want, or step through with me.

Operating margin

1. Move to the formula cell.   Move to B12.
2. Start the formula.   Type =
3. Select the first input cell.   Click on B5.
4. Type the operation sign.   Type the subtraction sign -
5. Select the next input cell.   Click on B10.
6. Continue selecting cells until you've finished.
7. Enter the formula.   **Enter**

   Answer: **17**

Do it now!

© 1998 Adkins & Matchett   **37**

BUILD BUSINESS SPREADSHEETS USING EXCEL

Net income

1. Move to B14.
2. Type =
3. Click on B12.
4. Type the subtraction sign -
5. Click on B13.
6. **Enter**.

   Answer: **3**

The final result

	A	B
1	Formula practice 1	
2		
3	Sales	140
4	Expenses	100
5	Gross margin	40
6		
7	Selling expenses	10
8	Supplies	5
9	Overhead	8
10	Total operating expenses	23
11		
12	Operating margin	17
13	Non-operating expenses	14
14	Net income	3

= B3 - B4 (row 5)
= B7 + B8 + B9 (row 10)
= B5 - B10 (row 12)
= B11 - B12 (row 14)

What if?

Congratulations! You just created an income statement. Now do what the business world does: experiment.

What is net income if....

a. ☐ Sales are 150? *(find out, then change Sales back to 140)*

b. ☐ Non-operating expenses are 18? *(change back to 14 when you have the answer)*

c. ☐ Selling expenses drop to 7? *(change back to 10 when you have the answer)*

   Answers: a. 13, b. -1, c. 6

Save your spreadsheet as **P&L**.

Training for Finance

PART 1. FOUNDATION SKILLS

EXERCISE 7 ▶ Build a spreadsheet

Exercise 7: Build spreadsheets

Remember, this is business. You're building something your boss can use and approve of. So make sure each spreadsheet is complete.

Standards
- List every input so your boss can see it.
- Use cell references in each formula. Otherwise your boss's what-if games won't work and you'll look bad.

If you like, put each spreadsheet on a different sheet in the same file.

1. **Find total property, plant and equipment (PP&E) costs from these inputs:**

Land	14000
Buildings	98000
Equipment	147000

   Total PP&E: [ ]

   What - If
   What is Total PP&E if Land is 17500 and Equipment is 194600?

   [ ]

2. **Find retained earnings from these inputs:**

Last year's retained earnings	4010
This year's net income	880
This year's dividend payout	220

   This year's ret. earnings [ ]   *Hint: last yr + net inc - div payout*

   What - If
   What if dividends are raised to 300?

   This year's ret. earnings [ ]

   > **Note** If you've done the Adkins & Matchett *Introduction to Accounting for Finance* workbook: This is a **BASE** analysis problem!

3. **Find cost of goods sold (COGS) if sales are 400 and you assume COGS to be 70% of sales.**

   COGS [ ]

   COGS at 65% of sales [ ]

© 1998 Adkins & Matchett

BUILD BUSINESS SPREADSHEETS USING EXCEL

Do it now!

TIP: Empty cells in formulas

Suppose you are building a spreadsheet and you don't know one of your input numbers yet. Can you leave that input cell empty and build formulas that refer to it, then fill in the number later?

Try it and see.

Most formulas work. But try dividing a number by an empty cell and see what happens.

Ranges

Before you move on, you need to know what a range is. A range is a block of cells. It can be one cell or many, many cells. Ranges are always rectangles.

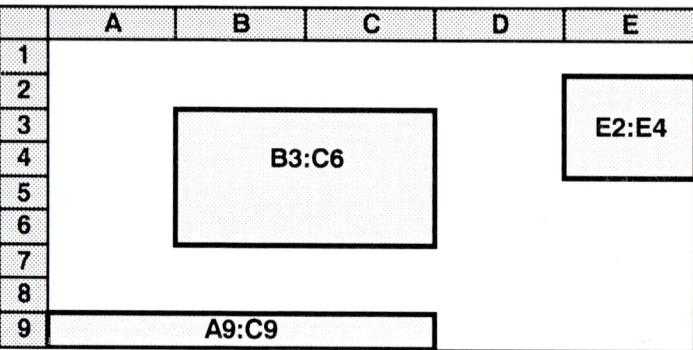

	A	B	C	D	E
1					
2					E2:E4
3		B3:C6			
4					
5					
6					
7					
8					
9	A9:C9				

Examples of ranges

Ranges are written the way you see them in the diagram.

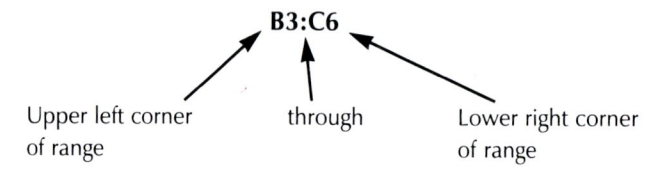

B3:C6

Upper left corner of range   through   Lower right corner of range

Now you're going to learn about a very powerful feature: *functions*.

40 Training for Finance

PART 1. FOUNDATION SKILLS

INTRODUCTION TO FUNCTIONS

So far, you've "custom made" all your formulas. Excel has many standard "off the shelf" formulas, called functions, that perform operations ranging from very simple to horribly complex. Functions are extremely useful and you should learn how to use the most common ones.

The SUM function

Your first function is the **SUM** function, a convenient way to add up long strings of numbers.

Because it's used so much, the **SUM** function has its own icon Σ and its own special keyboard shortcut.

Use the SUM function

Do it now!

Set up this spreadsheet:

	A	B
1	Budget	
2	Salaries	6540
3	Benefits	2420
4	Overhead	1100
5	Supplies	988
6	Travel and entertainment	1150
7	Total	

Hint: Indent the Total line by hitting the space bar 3 – 4 times. Crude, but it works.

You could create a formula that adds **B2+B3+B4+B5+B6**, but that's a long, time-consuming process. The **SUM** function was built for just such situations, so use it instead.

1. Place your cursor on the formula cell.   Move to **B7.**

2. Call up the **SUM** function.   **ALT =**
   Click the Σ icon.

3. Check the function's automatic selection. *Look at the wiggling box that forms around the nearest number cells. It should surround B2 – B6.*

4. Enter the function into the cell.   **ENTER**

The SUM shortcut

BEST PRACTICES

Use the **SUM** function keyboard shortcut: **ALT =**

My personal favorite!

© 1998 Adkins & Matchett 41

BUILD BUSINESS SPREADSHEETS USING EXCEL

The SUM function and ranges

Put the pointer on B7 and look at the **Edit Bar**.

Notice that the **SUM** function looks different from a handmade formula:

=SUM(B2:B6)

Instead of showing each cell individually, the SUM function shows you a range of cells.

=**SUM(B2:B6)** means "Add up cells B2 through B6." It includes all the cells between B2 and B6. Very efficient!

EXERCISE 8 ▶ SUM function

Exercise 8: SUM workout

Use the **SUM** function

1. Use **SUM** functions to add the subtotals in this exercise.

    Create your own formula for *Total assets* by adding *Total current assets* and *Total non-current assets*.

	A	B	C
1	Assets	Last year	This year
2			
3	Cash	350	370
4	Accounts receivable	840	790
5	Inventory	475	490
6	Total current assets		
7			
8	Net PP&E	1440	1470
9	Intangibles	900	705
10	Other	140	155
11	Total non-current assets		
12			
13	Total assets		

2. What will *Total assets* be this year if …

    This year's cash is **400** AND

    This year's inventory is **480** AND

    This year's intangibles are **1044**?

Training for Finance

Formula review

1. **Formulas always begin with =**

    When you write a formula,
    a. the result of the calculation appears in the formula cell
    b. the formula itself appears in the Edit Bar

2. **Review of formula construction**

    =   Start the formula with the special symbol that tells Excel "This is a formula"

    Click on input cell

    Operation sign

    Click on next input cell

    ENTER

What can go wrong?

The most common errors people make when they're writing formulas:

- They don't start with =   **B14+B15**

- They forget the multiplication sign.   **=B4(B6-B2)**

- They move the pointer too much before entering the formula. When the pointer moves, the cell reference moves, too.

    Beginning: **=A12+B12**

    Instead of entering the formula, Person X moves the mouse, and suddenly the formula reads **=A12+C14** or something else that isn't what they want.

- They press **ENTER** before they've finished building the formula.

- They type an operation sign after the last cell reference: **=B6+B12+**

- They refer to a cell which contains text or other non-numeric input. Excel will send you a **#VALUE!** message, which means: "I need a value to compute this formula, and one of your inputs isn't a value!"

- They drag the mouse when they click on a cell. Instead of getting one cell, they get a range of cells: **=B4*C6:C7**. The formula will still work, but anyone who is trying to make sense of your spreadsheet will be confused about your intentions.

FIND OUT FOR YOURSELF
Make deliberate errors.

Try each error for yourself and see what happens. Don't bother to type numbers into the cells. You'll get the same errors using blank cells.

BUILD BUSINESS SPREADSHEETS USING EXCEL

EXERCISE 9
Formula and SUM review

Exercise 9: Formula and SUM function review

Now put all your skills to work.

Clear your screen.   **ALT f c**

1. Set up the following spreadsheet and prepare to fill in the boxes with working formulas and functions.

	A	B
1	Budget	
2		
3	Inflation index	5%
4	Benefits as % of salaries	40%
5		
6	Salaries	4670
7	Benefits	
8	Overhead	1120
9	Supplies	675
10	Travel & entertainment	2355
11	Budget	
12		
13	Inflation amount	
14	Adjusted budget	

2. First calculate the benefits amount. Notice the benefits are 40% of salaries (Row 3).

3. Now calculate the budget before inflation is added.

4. Calculate the inflation amount (5% of the total budget).

5. Add the inflation amount to the total budget to get the adjusted budget.

What-If No. 1

What will the adjusted budget be if …

   … inflation is actually 3%?

What-If No. 2

What will the adjusted budget be if…

   … inflation is 5% and benefits are 45% of salary?

44 Training for Finance

PART 1. FOUNDATION SKILLS

PAPER & PENCIL EXERCISE

Test #3

How much do you know about formulas?

1. Which of the following shows a range?
   - ☐ B3, C16
   - ☐ D44:E52
   - ☐ AZ242+BA361

2. You should always use cell references in formulas so that …
   - ☐ You can play "What-If" games later
   - ☐ Key numbers like a 5% inflation rate are visible on the spreadsheet instead of being buried in a formula
   - ☐ Both of the above

3. You can indent subtotal labels by

4. Which of these formulas won't work, and why?
   a. =B4(C11+D14)
   b. =D8+D9-C12+
   c. =SUM(C14:D19)

5. Cells used in a formula cannot be empty.
   - ☐ True
   - ☐ False

6. Write formulas to go in the boxed cells below. You should be able to do this without using Excel.

	A	B
1	Budget	
2		
3	Salaries	3200
4	Benefits	1184
5	Overhead	900
6	Supplies	775
7	Budget	6059
8		
9	Benefits % of salary	
10	Salary as % of total budget	

© 1998 Adkins & Matchett   45

BUILD BUSINESS SPREADSHEETS USING EXCEL

E. THE COPY COMMAND

- Select more than one cell
- Copy data
- Copy formulas

Select groups of cells

You can apply one command to a number of different cells by using selection techniques.

Do it now!

Select and erase

If you have data on your screen, prepare to erase it in one operation.

Hold down **SHIFT**. Move the pointer by using the arrow keys and see what happens.

Drag the mouse over several cells *(Hint: hold down the left mouse button as you move the mouse)* and see what happens.

What happens when you select with the mouse, hold down **SHIFT**, and select some more?

Do it now!

Put selections to work: erase ranges

You're going to erase all your previous work, so make sure you don't want to save any of it. (You won't need it in any other exercise.)

Select a few cells that have formulas and input data in them. Now press **Delete** to get rid of all of them at once.

Experiment with keyboard selection and mouse selection. Keep selecting and deleting until you've gotten rid of everything on your sheet.

BEST PRACTICES

The copy command

OK, enough fooling around! Let's get to an essential feature of Excel that you'll use every time you make a spreadsheet: the copy command.

Excel offers you a number of different ways to copy. I'm going to show you the expert way first. Later I'll give you alternatives and you can decide if you want to use one of them instead.

First, open the **Edit** menu.

Notice the **Copy** command. Written on the right is a keyboard shortcut that the pros use: **CTRL C**

Escape twice to get back to the spreadsheet.

46 Training for Finance

PART 1. FOUNDATION SKILLS

COPY

Type your name in Cell A1 and copy it.

Step 1. Move to the "original" cell that you want to copy.	1. Go to Cell A1 and enter your name.
Step 2. Copy	2. Hold down **CTRL and tap C.**
	Notice the wiggling box around A1. It shows what you've copied.
Step 3. Move to the cell(s) where you want to place the copy.	3. Move to Cell A2.
Step 4. Paste the copy into place.	4. **Enter**

How copying works

Copying is a two-part process.

First: You copy something into an invisible area called the **clipboard**. Now you have two copies of the information: the original copy on the spreadsheet, and an exact copy on the **clipboard**.

Second: You **paste** the clipboard copy into a new area on the spreadsheet. The original is not changed in any way.

When you issued the **CTRL C** command, you copied your name onto the clipboard.

When you **ENTER**ed, you pasted the **clipboard** copy into the spreadsheet.

Practice

Practice copying your name until you're comfortable with the **Copy** command.

Copy one cell to a selection

Do it now!

Delete everything you've put on the sheet except your name in Cell **A1**.

Move back to your name in **A1**. **Copy** it.

Select the row of cells in **B1** through **E1**. *Quick review: Hold down the SHIFT key. Tap the right arrow key until you've selected B1 through E1. Or use the mouse.*

ENTER

Practice

Do it now!

Copy your name to a column of five cells.

Copy your name to a block of cells 4 rows deep and 4 columns wide.

Select all the copied cells and delete them.

© 1998 Adkins & Matchett

BUILD BUSINESS SPREADSHEETS USING EXCEL

Copy a row or column of cells

Do it now!

Type something new in Cell **A1**.

Copy it across from **B1** to **F1**.

Now **select the entire row of copies** (**A1** through **F1**).

Copy it down to **A2** through **F2**.

Create a column of data and copy it to another column.

FIND OUT FOR YOURSELF

Can you "jump" across empty cells to copy to a distant cell? Try it and see. Copy **A1** to **D12**.

Copy formulas

Copying data is fun, but the real payoff comes when you copy formulas.

If you feel shaky about the copy command, stop and practice it some more before you move on to this next section. You're going to need your brain cells free to understand what happens next.

Set up formulas

Do it now!

Set up the following spreadsheet:

	A	B	C
1		Last year	This year
2	Admin costs	30	35
3	Salary	40	42
4	Total operating expenses		

Create a formula

Go to Cell **B4** and create this formula to add these expenses:

   =B2 + B3

The **SUM** function would work just fine here, but I think this example will be clearer if you use the cell-by-cell formula.

You need exactly the same formula in Column C for this year's expenses. Can you copy the formula for last year and get the answer for this year?

Training for Finance

PART 1. FOUNDATION SKILLS

Copy the formula

Use your copying skills to copy the formula in **B4** to **C4**.

The magic of the Copy command

The original formula reads **=B2 + B3**. The copy reads **=C2 + C3**. The formula adjusted itself automatically. How?

When you copy a formula, the **Copy** command normally copies the cell pattern, not the cell addresses themselves.

The pattern of the formula you just copied is: 2-cells-up plus 1-cell-up. That pattern works for Column C's formula cell too.

KEY KNOWLEDGE

The Copy command normally copies a pattern, not exact cell addresses.

Do it again...

Add to your spreadsheet.

	A	B	C
1		Last year	This year
2	Admin costs	30	35
3	Salary	40	42
4	Total operating expenses	70	77
5			
6	Interest expenses	12	12
7	Other	4	5
8	Non-operating expenses		

Use the **SUM** function to add the two non-operating expenses in Cell **B8**. Then copy the formula to **C8**.

The copy command works on functions, too.

EXERCISE 10 ▶
Copy formulas & SUM functions: Review

Exercise 10: Copy formulas and SUM functions: Review

1. Set up the following spreadsheet and save it as SALES.

	A	B	C	D	E	F
1	Sales performance					
2						Individual
3		Qtr 1	Qtr 2	Qtr 3	Qtr 4	totals
4	Ancona	460	340	380	370	SUM
5	Baker	200	300	400	450	COPY
6	Casey	375	325	500	450	COPY
7	Daggett	500	600	500	650	COPY
8	Quarterly totals	SUM	COPY	COPY	COPY	

2. Fill in the **SUM** function for quarterly totals and copy it across.

3. Fill in the **SUM** function for individual totals and copy it down.

What are total 4th quarter sales? (Cell **E8**) ☐

What-If
What will be Daggett's total sales if her sales in Qtr 2 are 629 instead of 600 and in the 4th quarter are 717 instead of 650?

☐

© 1998 Adkins & Matchett

BUILD BUSINESS SPREADSHEETS USING EXCEL

PAPER & PENCIL EXERCISE

Projection: an informed guess about the future!

Your job may require you to create lots of them!

Test #4

Your first projection

You're going to tackle the most complex spreadsheet you've seen yet. But you've already performed every task it requires, so you should be able to create this one with no problems.

This spreadsheet is a **projection**, a very common type of business spreadsheet. You're projecting the income statement accounts for four quarters. Since everything's taking place in the future, you're building your projection on assumptions.

The spreadsheet is also simplified. You'll be building more realistic projections in Part 2.

1. Set up the following spreadsheet and save it as INCSTATE.

	A	B	C	D	E
1	Assumptions	Qtr 1	Qtr 2	Qtr 3	Qtr 4
2	COGS % of sales	70%	65%	68%	65%
3	Op. expenses % of sales	22%	24%	23%	24%
4	Other expenses % of sales	4%	3%	4%	5%
5					
6	Income statement				
7	Sales	600	650	590	680
8	COGS				
9	Gross margin				
10					
11	Operating expenses				
12	Non-operating expenses				
13	Total expenses				
14					
15	Net income				

2. First, calculate the accounts and the subtotals.

   *Hint: Notice that the other accounts are all dependent on sales. To calculate each account, multiply sales * the percentage for that account in the assumption block.*

   Hint: For the subtotals:

Gross margin:	Sales - COGS
Total expenses:	Op. expenses + Non-op. expenses
Net income:	Gross margin - Total expenses

3. Next, copy the formulas across. You can copy them one at a time or all together.

4. What is Net income in the 4th quarter?

   What is Net income in the 4th quarter if 4th quarter COGS rises to 68% and Op. expenses rises to 25%?

5. Save this file as INCSTATE.

50   Training for Finance

PART 1. FOUNDATION SKILLS

F. MOVING THINGS AROUND

- Cut and paste (move)
- Select rows or columns
- Manipulate rows and columns
- Insert and delete cells

You must know how to move things around: data, rows, columns, and even individual cells.

Moving data around

The Cut command

Do it now!

**Cut
CTRL X**

CTRL X

Use the **Cut** command when you want to move data. **Cut** moves the contents of a cell, not the cell itself.

Like the **Copy** command, the **Cut** command comes in two parts.

1. **Cut** places a copy on the clipboard.

   When you **ENTER**, the copy pastes into your new location and the original disappears.

2. The **Cut** command is on the **Edit** menu. Use the keyboard shortcut **CTRL X**.

Try it!

HOW TO

CUT or MOVE	
1. Place pointer on cell(s) you want to move.	1. Put the cursor on **A1**.
2. Issue the **Cut** command.	2. **CTRL X**
3. Move to the cell where you want the data to appear.	3. Move to Cell **B3**.
4. Paste the data in place.	4. **ENTER**

Clear the screen and enter your name in Cell **A1**.

KEY KNOWLEDGE

To Paste multiple copies, use CTRL V

Two ways to Paste

So far you've Pasted by using **Enter**. You can Paste multiple copies of the clipboard by using **CTRL V** instead of **ENTER**. Try it. Notice the wiggling box stays on the screen, telling you that the copy is still on the clipboard. Press **ENTER** or **Esc** to get rid of the wiggling box.

© 1998 Adkins & Matchett   51

BUILD BUSINESS SPREADSHEETS USING EXCEL

Do it now!

Practice

Enter various labels and numbers and practice moving them to new locations.

Cut the following:

- ☐ Single cells
- ☐ Ranges

Using Cut with formulas

Now for the tricky part.

What happens when you **Cut** and **Paste** a formula or function? Try the next exercise and find out.

EXERCISE 11 ▶ MOVE it!

Exercise 11: MOVE (Cut)

1. Open INCSTATE (or go back to Test #4 on if you didn't create it then).

	A	B	C	D	E
1	Assumptions	Qtr 1	Qtr 2	Qtr 3	Qtr 4
2	COGS % of sales	70%	65%	68%	65%
3	Op. expenses % of sales	22%	24%	23%	24%
4	Other expenses % of sales	4%	3%	4%	5%
5					
6	Income statement				
7	Sales	600	650	590	680
8	COGS	420	422.5	401.2	442
9	Gross margin	180	227.5	188.8	238
10					
11	Operating expenses	132	156	135.7	163.2
12	Other expenses	24	19.5	23.6	34
13	Total expenses	156	175.5	159.3	197.2
14					
15	Net income	24	52	29.5	40.8

All of the cells from B8 through E15 should be formulas. Check your work and redo it if you have simply typed numbers into place.

2. Move the COGS formula in **E8** to Cell **F8**.

   Click on **E8**
   CTRL X
   Click on **F8**
   ENTER

   The formula still works accurately! Check the cell references. They still refer to Column **E** even though the formula is in Column **F**.

   Even better: check the formula in Gross margin, cell **E9**. The cell reference automatically adjusted to refer to the COGS cell's new address.

3. Move the COGS formula back to its old position and recheck the cell references in both COGS and Gross margin. They've automatically changed again!

KEY KNOWLEDGE

When you move an entry, formulas adjust to its new position automatically

52 Training for Finance

PART 1. FOUNDATION SKILLS

The **Cut** feature is a powerful tool. You can use it knowing that any formulas that depend on the moved cell have automatically adjusted themselves.

Do it now!

Try this challenge

With the COGS formula back in its original position, try this experiment.

1. **Copy** (not **Cut**) the COGS formula from **E8** to **F8**. The copy says 0. Why?
   Hint: Look at the cell references in the copy.

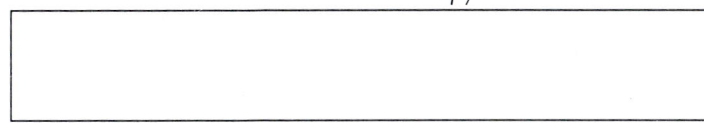

   Answer: There are no assumptions or sales in F2 through F7, so the formulas can't calculate properly.

   When you're finished, close INCSTATE without saving it.

Do it now!
SHIFT space
CTRL space

2. Get ready to manipulate entire rows and columns

   You can select entire rows or columns. This means from the top to the bottom of the spreadsheet.

Row:	SHIFT spacebar	Click on row number
Column:	CTRL spacebar	Click on column letter

Try it

Clear the screen if anything is on it.   **ALT f c**   then   **ALT f n**

Type something in any cell in Columns **B**, **C**, and **D**.

Now select whole columns and rows. Try out both the keyboard and the mouse.

What happens if you hit **Delete** when a whole row is selected? Experiment.

Moving rows and columns

Select an entire row. *(See the selection tips, above)*

Cut it.

Paste it elsewhere. ***Watch out!*** The pasted copy will "write over" anything in its way.

WARNING

Try it
Try moving an entire column.

© 1998 Adkins & Matchett

BUILD BUSINESS SPREADSHEETS USING EXCEL

Do it now!

Insert row / column
ALT i r / c

Insert rows *(columns work the same way)*

You can insert rows or columns anywhere you like. There are several methods:

Method 1.   Select first
Select the row where you want the new row inserted.
SHIFT spacebar
Then insert.
Press **CTRL +**. Use the + key on the number pad.

or

Method 2.   Give the command first.
Place your pointer where you want the new row to appear.
Give the Insert rows command.
CTRL + (use the number pad + key)
Select **Entire Row** from the dialog box.

or

Method 3.   Use the menu. ALT i r

Do it now!

Find out for yourself

What happens to formulas when you insert a row?
 1. Create the following example:

	A	B	C
1		1	
2		2	
3		3	
4			

 2. Create a **SUM** function in Cell **B4**.

 3. Put the pointer on Row 3. and insert a new row.

 4. What happens to the **SUM** function?

   Answer: It automatically includes the new row.

KEY KNOWLEDGE
Excel adjusts formulas when you insert rows

Do it now!

Delete row
ALT e d r

Delete column
ALT e d c

Delete rows (columns, too)

SHIFT spacebar, then CTRL –
   or

Place your pointer anywhere in the row you want to delete.
CTRL –   Select **Entire Row** from the dialog box.

ALT e d r

54 Training for Finance

PART 1. FOUNDATION SKILLS

What happens if you delete rows a formula uses?

1. Delete Row 2.

   Notice that the **SUM** function can handle the situation. It adjusts automatically.

2. Restore the deleted row with **CTRL Z**.

3. Add another formula:

	A	B	
1		1	
2		2	
3		3	
4		6	=SUM(B1:B3)
5			
6		2	=B1 * B2

   Move to Cell **B6** and multiply **B1 * B2**.

4. Now delete Row 2.

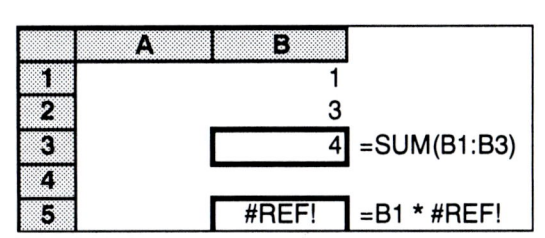

	A	B	
1		1	
2		3	
3		4	=SUM(B1:B3)
4			
5		#REF!	=B1 * #REF!

OH NO!

The **SUM** function could handle the deletion, but the formula in **B6** (now **B5**) couldn't.

Check the **Edit Bar** to see what's in the formula. The formula has "lost its head" and doesn't know what you want it to multiply any longer.

WARNING

Find out more about #REF! messages in Appendix H!

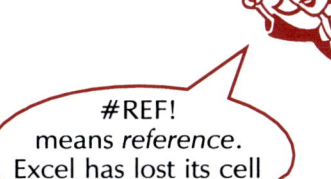

#REF! messages

You've just seen one of the worst messages you can get when you're working with a spreadsheet!

#REF! appears only in formula cells. It means the formula has lost one of its references. You have to either **Undo** what you've just done by using **CTRL Z** or yo have to stop and rebuild the formula by hand.

#REF! messages invalidate your entire spreadsheet, so you can't just ignore them.

#REF! means reference. Excel has lost its cell reference!

Find out for yourself

Can you also get **#REF!** messages by deleting columns?

> Select a column with the mouse or **CTRL spacebar**.
> Then use **CTRL –** or **ALT e d c** to delete the column.

© 1998 Adkins & Matchett **55**

BUILD BUSINESS SPREADSHEETS USING EXCEL

In depth

If you delete the row or column instead of the contents of their cells, what happens to the spreadsheet overall?

Two things happen:

The contents of the row or column's cells disappear, and

A new row is added to the bottom of the spreadsheet, or a column is added on the far right side.

So the spreadsheet doesn't lose any rows or columns in total, although the row or column you delete gets squeezed into oblivion.

Find out for yourself

Contrast the difference between deleting the contents of a column or row by using the **Delete** key and deleting the entire column or row.

PAPER & PENCIL EXERCISE

Test #5: Copy, Move, Delete

Look at the spreadsheet below.

	A	B	C
1			
2	Base price	100	200
3	Markup %	50%	50%
4	Markup	50	100
5	Selling price	150	

Base + markup

1. If you copy the formula in the box to **C5**, what will appear in **C5**?
   ☐ 150   ☐ 300

2. If you move the formula in the box to **C5**, what will appear in **C5**?
   ☐ 150   ☐ 300

Look at this spreadsheet:

	A	B
1		
2	Base price	100
3	Markup %	50%
4	Markup	50
5	Selling price	150

=B2 + B4

3. What will appear in Cell **B5** if you delete Row **2**?
   ☐ #REF!   ☐ 50

continued on next page

continued from previous page

Examine this spreadsheet:

	A	B
1		
2	Subsidiary A	400
3	Subsidiary B	200
4	Subsidiary C	100
5	Total worth	700 =SUM(B2:B4)

4. What will the SUM function read if you delete Row 3?
   ☐ #REF!   ☐ 500

5. What does the **#REF!** message mean?

   [   ]

6. **#REF!** messages are
   ☐ not too bad   ☐ very serious

BUILD BUSINESS SPREADSHEETS USING EXCEL

G. PRESENTATION

- Icons, toolbars, and help
- Selecting toolbars
- Formatting cells

ICONS, TOOLBARS, AND HELP

- Using icons
- Installing and de-installing toolbars
- Getting help

Using icons

I've been teaching you keyboard commands so far, but sometimes icons are easier to use. It's time for you to learn your way around the icon bar if you haven't already done so.

Which icon does what?

Move the mouse pointer to an icon and let it rest there without clicking it. After a moment you'll see a little pop-up box that tells you what the icon does.

Do it now!

Try it Explore the icon bar until you find the icons for these tasks:
  SUM function   "AutoSum"
  List of functions   "FunctionWizard"
  Copy
  Paste

Getting help

You can get help several different ways:

  F1

  or **ALT H**

  Help icon

Do it now!

Try it now. Look for help on *"functions, worksheet."* Go to *"About Worksheet Functions"* and look through this section.

58 Training for Finance

PART 1. FOUNDATION SKILLS

Help for functions

Place your pointer on an empty cell. Then use Function Paste *(Excel 97)* / Function Wizard *(earlier versions of Excel)* to look at Excel's lists of functions.

ALT i f

Click the Function icon.

Notice that the functions are grouped in lists.

Help for the SUM function

Select the **Math & Trig** category.

Select the **SUM** function from the list. *Shortcut: Tab to or click the Function Name list and type S until you find the SUM function.*

Some people find this next screen less than totally helpful. A better explanation of the function will appear if you use the button that calls up Help or the Office assistant on this screen. Then you can look at examples.

BEST PRACTICES

Whenever you're learning about a new function, go to the Function icon's Help or Office Assistant button to see examples of the function in use.

Structure of a function

All functions have the same general structure: =NAME(arguments).

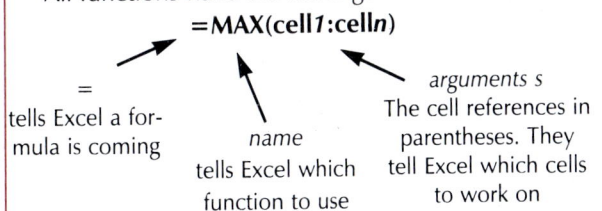

=MAX(cell1:celln)

= tells Excel a formula is coming

name tells Excel which function to use

arguments The cell references in parentheses. They tell Excel which cells to work on

Find out for yourself

Do it now!

1. Can the **SUM** function add up as many as 50 *separate* cells ("arguments")?
   ☐ Yes ☐ No

2. Look up the **COUNT** function. It's in the Statistical category. Look at the Help screen for **COUNT**. Are **COUNT**'s arguments like **SUM**'s?
   ☐ Yes ☐ No

   Answers: 1. No   2. Yes

© 1998 Adkins & Matchett   **59**

BUILD BUSINESS SPREADSHEETS USING EXCEL

NUMBER FORMATTING

Set up your toolbars for formatting

Right now you're probably looking at the standard Excel toolbar. You need the formatting toolbar for this section. Here's how to get it:

ALT View Toolbars

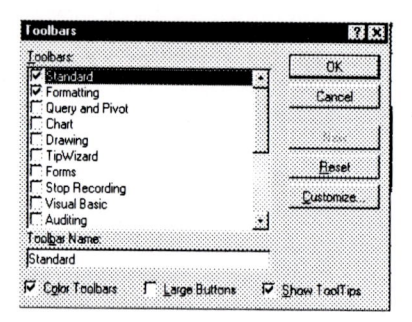

Select **Formatting** and **ENTER**.

Do it now!

Use your right mouse button to click on any icon. You should get a pop-up menu that looks like this:

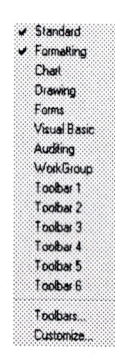

Click on **Formatting** to put a check mark beside it.
ENTER

Now you have two toolbars on the screen.

Get rid of extra toolbars

Do it now!

If you need to get rid of a toolbar, go back to the toolbar menu. Click a toolbar's name to make the check mark go away.

Look in the Appendix for more info

See Appendix D to learn more about different toolbars and how to customize them.

Training for Finance

PART 1. FOUNDATION SKILLS

Formatting: the bottomless pit of time wasting

Formatting is the least important aspect of creating a spreadsheet, but it often takes the most time. You can get carried away creating little boxes and shadows; you can experiment with changing font colors; you can waste hours of precious time fooling around with arrows and text boxes, and none of it will affect what really counts in your spreadsheet: structure and accuracy.

WARNING

Like cosmetics

Formatting is like cosmetics. It's a surface change that can be helpful. My advice to you about formatting is:

- Keep it tasteful, simple and plain.
- If you have an extra hour to spend on your spreadsheet, spend it checking and proofreading your formulas, not on fancy formatting.
- If you find yourself spending more than a few minutes on formatting, you're probably wasting your time.

Currency and comma formats

Stop using Automatic formatting now!

It's time to stop using Automatic number formatting (typing the formatting as you enter a number). If you want to format a number, use the currency and comma icons on the Formatting toolbar that you installed earlier.

Read Appendix D to learn more precise ways of controlling formats.

Use the icons

Do it now!

Experiment with the currency **$** and comma **,** icons. Use the **Increase Decimals** and **Decrease Decimals** icons to control decimal places.

What happens to negative numbers?

How negative numbers appear :

Comma icon	(20)
Currency icon	$ (20)
General format (no format)	-20

Most business people use parentheses to show negative numbers as they are easier to see. An exception to this rule is percentages, which can appear either with or without parentheses.

KEY KNOWLEDGE

Show negative numbers in parentheses

Percent formats

You can also use the percent format. Remember, if you change the number 1 to percent format, it will read 100%. Excel 97 operates a little differently. If you type 1, it will convert the number to 1%, not 100%.

© 1998 Adkins & Matchett   **61**

BUILD BUSINESS SPREADSHEETS USING EXCEL

Do it now!

Change the number of decimal places

Type **4.049** in an empty, unformatted cell.

Find the Decrease Decimals icon and click it once.

You should see **4.05** in the cell.

Did you actually change the number? Check by looking at the **Edit Bar**. You'll see the full value of the number in the **Edit Bar**.

Click Decrease Decimals again, then again. Check the **Edit Bar** each time.

Now use the Increase Decimals icon to increase the number of decimal places you can see.

Formatting and calculation

How does formatting affect the calculation of a formula? It doesn't. Excel calculates with the full value of the number no matter what the format shows.

The example below will demonstrate everything.

Do it now!

What number does Excel calculate with?

Try this:

1. Input these numbers.

	A	B
1	4.049	4
2	3.049	3

2. Select all four cells. Format them to show one decimal place *(click the Comma icon, then click Increase Decimals icon)*.

	A	B
1	4.0	4.0
2	3.0	3.0

   The numbers look exactly the same, don't they?

3. Add each column and see what happens.

	A	B
1	4.0	4.0
2	3.0	3.0
3	7.1	7.0

Notice that the rounding effect of the decimal places makes the answer look wrong. Excel is calculating with the full value of the cells, not the formatted appearance.

KEY KNOWLEDGE

Changing the format of a number does not change its actual value. Excel calculates with the full value of the number even if you don't see any decimal places.

PART 1. FOUNDATION SKILLS

Problems with formatting

You will see these entries from time to time:

#######

1E+08

These entries are not really problems when you understand what they are and how to deal with them.

"Hash" in cells

Enter the number 12345.6789 in an empty cell. *(In Excel 97, make sure there's another short entry someplace in the same column.)* Increase the number of decimal points until the number is too big to fit in the cell. What happens?

Decrease the decimal points until you see the number again.

Now change the number to Currency format. Do you get the problem again?

Whenever you see a cell full of hash that looks like this,

	A
1	
2	#######

the format of the number is too big to fit in the cell. Either there are too many decimal places or you have used a format like Currency or Comma, which adds extras like commas, decimal places, and a currency sign.

It's only a cosmetic problem. Formulas still calculate the hashed cell correctly. But you wouldn't want to show an unreadable spreadsheet to anyone.

Either widen the column or adjust the formatting.

> In Excel 97, the column will adjust automatically if there are no other entries in it

Scientific notation 1E+08

Excel converts very large or very small numbers to scientific notation if the number has never been formatted.

Most business spreadsheets never use scientific notation, so you should do something about the problem if it occurs. You have 3 choices:

- **Widen the column**
- **Change the scale of the number**
- **Format the number**

KEY KNOWLEDGE

Excel converts very large or very small numbers to scientific notation only if they are not formatted

© 1998 Adkins & Matchett   **63**

BUILD BUSINESS SPREADSHEETS USING EXCEL

TEXT FORMATTING

Use either text formatting icons or keyboard shortcuts to format text.

Bold, italics, underscore

CTRL B	Bold on/off
CTRL I	Italics on/on
CTRL U	Underscore on/off

Use icons on the formatting toolbar.

Center, left and right alignment

Use the toolbar icons to center text or shift it to the left or right.

Yes, there are keyboard commands that will align text, but they are much longer and more cumbersome than the icons. You'll learn them later.

Don't center or left align numbers! Apply the alignment icons only to words. It would be a very rare day when you would want to change the alignment of numbers from right justified to anything else.

Try it

Open INCSTATE and dress it up. Use the right alignment icon, **CTRL B**, the Comma icon, and the Increase Decimals icons to make it look like this:

	A	B	C	D	E
1	Assumptions	Qtr 1	Qtr 2	Qtr 3	Qtr 4
2	COGS % of sales	70.0%	65.0%	68.0%	65.0%
3	Op. expenses % of sales	22.0%	24.0%	23.0%	24.0%
4	Other expenses % of sales	4.0%	3.0%	4.0%	5.0%
5					
6	Income statement				
7	Sales	600.0	650.0	590.0	680.0
8	COGS	420.0	422.5	401.2	442.0
9	Gross margin	180.0	227.5	188.8	238.0
10					
11	Operating expenses	132.0	156.0	135.7	163.2
12	Non-operating expenses	24.0	19.5	23.6	34.0
13	Total expenses	156.0	175.5	159.3	197.2
14					
15	Net income	24.0	52.0	29.5	40.8

Now type 600 in cell B2. Notice how the percent format remains. Even if you delete the cell contents, the formatting "sticks." You would have to reformat the cell to change the formatting.

Change B2 back to 70.0% and save INCSTATE again.

KEY KNOWLEDGE
Cells "remember" their formatting until you change it

Training for Finance

PART 1. FOUNDATION SKILLS

MOUSE MENUS AND OPTIONS

Mouse vs. keyboard

OK, it's time for you to explore the mouse menus. You may decide you want to use the mouse for more commands. Although I (and most power users) think the keyboard shortcuts are the fastest, most efficient way to make Excel do what you want, you may feel more comfortable using the mouse.

So here are some mouse alternatives and commands.

Do it now!

Mouse menus

Spreadsheet mouse menu

Click the right mouse button in the spreadsheet.

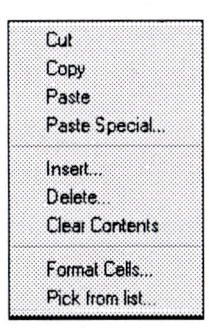

```
Cut
Copy
Paste
Paste Special...

Insert...
Delete...
Clear Contents

Format Cells...
Pick from list...
```

This little menu offers alternative ways to get to **Cut**, **Copy** and more.

Try using the commands on this menu to see if you really fall in love with the mouse. I think it's slow, slooow, slooooooooow....

WARNING

Be careful!

Delete... on this menu refers to cell, column and row delete. It's a dangerous command, so be sure you really want to use it.

Clear Contents is the equivalent of the **Delete** key. It erases the contents of a cell, not the cell itself. However, it does not erase any formatting you've applied.

KEY KNOWLEDGE

Be careful of the delete command on the mouse menu – it's not the same as the Delete key

Toolbar mouse menu

Click the right mouse button on any icon. You'll find a shortcut menu for the toolbars.

Sheet tab mouse menu

Click the right mouse button on the sheet tabs at the bottom of the spreadsheet (those little tabs that say Sheet1, Sheet2, Sheet3, and so on). The next section explains how to use these sheets and what the commands do to them.

© 1998 Adkins & Matchett

BUILD BUSINESS SPREADSHEETS USING EXCEL

MULTIPLE SHEETS

Workbook: Many spreadsheets in one

Look at the bottom edge of the spreadsheet and find the sheet tabs that say Sheet1, Sheet2, and so forth. Each of these sheets is a complete worksheet in itself.

Multiple sheets are useful for a number of purposes. Here are some typical ways they are used in business:

Financial statements	Each statement goes on its own sheet.
Quarterly sales records	Each quarter has its own sheet.
Divisions	Different divisions stay on their own sheets.
Fields	An oil company with several different oil fields might want to keep each field's records on a separate sheet.

Do it now!

Moving from sheet to sheet

- **CTRL Page Up** and **CTRL Page Down**
- Click on the sheet tab.

Number of sheets in a workbook

Normally, new workbooks have 8 or 16 sheets. You can add new sheets until you have up to 256 of them in the same workbook.

Getting to distant sheets

You may not be able to see all the sheet tabs at once. To get to distant sheets, try these options:

- Move from sheet to sheet rapidly with **CTRL Page Down / Up**

    or

- Use the mouse to click the arrows at the bottom right side of the spreadsheet.

Do it now!

The sheet arrows

Find out what the different arrows beside the sheet tabs do.

66 Training for Finance

PART 1. FOUNDATION SKILLS

KEY KNOWLEDGE

Keep your sheet names short. Don't use initials, especially with periods (I.S., B.S.). You'll be sorry later when you are trying to proofread formulas!

Name your sheets

Let's face it: **Sheet1** is not exactly an inspiring name. You should rename your sheets more expressively.

Two ways to rename your sheets:

ALT o h r

Double-click the sheet tab

or

Click the right mouse button on the sheet tab and use the sheet menu

You can use spaces and some punctuation in the sheet name. You can't use some punctuation marks in sheet names, like semicolons.

Do it now!

Rename those sheets

Go back to Sheet1.

Assume you own three companies named Gorp, Inc., Bladge Company, and Frisko Dog Treats. You're keeping their records on three sheets. Rename three sheets Gorp, Bladge, and Frisko.

If you don't like these names, make up some of your own!

Do it now!

Move sheets

The **mouse** is the best method for moving sheets.

Drag Frisko in front of Gorp and drop it.

Notice the little black arrowhead that moves along the sheet tabs when you drag. It shows you where the sheet will appear when you drop it.

Practice

Move Frisko in front of Gorp.

Move Gorp behind Bladge.

Delete or insert sheets

Use the mouse menu to insert or delete sheets.

Experiment with these commands now.

If you prefer the keyboard, try these commands:

Insert a sheet	ALT i w
Delete a sheet	ALT e l

© 1998 Adkins & Matchett

BUILD BUSINESS SPREADSHEETS USING EXCEL

PRINT

About printing

1. Print with **CTRL P**.

2. Always **Print Preview** before you print so you won't waste paper and time with unpleasant surprises.

3. Excel will print your entire spreadsheet unless you tell it not to.

BEST PRACTICES

Do it now!

**Preview
ALT f v**

Prepare to print a spreadsheet

Prepare to print the **BUDGET** spreadsheet. Make sure BUDGET is open.

Before you print, preview the spreadsheet.	**ALT f v**
Return to the spreadsheet	**Esc**
Print	**CTRL P**

See Appendix F for a full explanation of printing.

CHARTS

A note about charts. Sorry – they're not included in this workbook, which is big enough already. Charts are overdocumented in just about every standard book on Excel; they're pretty easy to do if you just play around with them. And they too often fall into the same category that formatting does: more sizzle than steak.

If charts are essential to your work with Excel, spend some time playing around with them with the Excel reference book in hand. You'll soon pick up everything you can and can't do with Excel charts.

TIPS: Select chart ranges before you start.

Try right mouse-button clicks in the chart to get to different editing commands.

If it gets hopelessly snarled up, it's often easier to simply throw away your attempt and start over again.

Training for Finance

PART 1. FOUNDATION SKILLS

FINAL TEST, PART 1

Let's see now...

Final Test

In all problems:
- Format dollars as dollars, other numbers with Comma format.
- Format percentages as percentages.

1. Set up spreadsheets to solve these problems:

   a. What interest will Billco pay on a debt of $65,000 if the annual interest rate is 7 1/2%?

   What if the interest rate is 9%?

   b.

2. a. Calculate the final sale price of a car if its dealer cost is $19,500 and the markup is 8%. *Hint: Final price = Dealer cost + markup*

   b. What if the dealer cost is $18,000 and the markup is 10%? What is the new sale price?

3. CopyCopyCo's most popular copier sells for $4995. CopyCopyCo pays $3475 for this copier. What is the profit margin?
   Hint: Divide the difference between cost and price by the price

4. Set up the following spreadsheet:

	A	B	C	D	E
1		Calculator	Laptop	Desktop	TOTALS
2	Price	$ 12.99	$2,499.95	$1,899.00	
3	Sales				
4	Week 1	460	65	34	
5	Week 2	350	60	15	
6	Week 3	420	55	40	
7	Total sales	1230	180	89	
8					
9	Gross sales				

Hint
Gross sales = price * total sales

Calculate the following:

Total laptops sold _____   Total items sold _____

Gross sales for all desktops _____   Gross sales for all items _____

continued on next page

© 1998 Adkins & Matchett **69**

BUILD BUSINESS SPREADSHEETS USING EXCEL

Hints

COGS	= Sales * COGS % of sales
Gross margin	= Sales − COGS
SG&A	= Sales * SG&A % of sales
Earn bef int. & tax	= Gross margin − SG&A

Taxes	= Earnings before int.
	  & taxes
	  * Taxes % of EBIT

Net income	= EBIT − Taxes

Scoring

1 a. 5 points _____
  b. 5 points _____
2 a. 5 points _____
  b. 5 points _____
3.   5 points _____
4.   20 points _____
5 a. 10 points _____
  b. 10 points _____
6.   5 points _____
7.   5 points _____
8.   5 points _____
9.   5 points _____
10.   5 points _____
11.   5 points _____
12.   5 points _____

YOUR TOTAL _____

out of a possible **100**

If you scored less than **90**, go back and review before moving to Part 2.

---

continued from previous page

5. Set up the following spreadsheet:

	A	B	C	D
1		Year 1	Year 2	Year 3
2	**Assumptions**			
3	COGS % of sales	62%	63%	64%
4	SG&A % of sales	24%	24%	25%
5	Taxes % of EBIT	37%	37%	37%
6				
7	**Income statement**			
8	Sales	850.0	975.0	1,125.0
9	COGS			
10	Gross margin			
11	SG&A			
12	Earnings bef. int. and taxes (EBIT)			
13	Taxes			
14	Net income			

Create formulas to complete the spreadsheet.

Format all whole numbers as comma with one decimal place.

Format percentages as percent with 0 decimal places.

a. What is Net income in Year 3?

   [   ]

b. If in Year 3 SG&A goes down to 23% and Sales go up to 1150, what will Net income be?

   [   ]

6. Suppose you see this ######## in a cell. What does it mean?

   [   ]

7. You format the number 4.3467 to 0 decimal places. Now it appears in the cell as 4.0. Which number does Excel calculate with?
   ☐ 4.3467   ☐ 4.0

8. What will happen to the formula =C4-C5 if you delete Row 5?
   ☐ =C4   ☐ =C4 − #REF!   ☐ Nothing: it will automatically adjust

9. If you insert a row, any formula referring to cells below that row will:
   ☐ show #REF!   ☐ automatically adjust itself   ☐ not change

10. If you cut a formula and move it to another cell, its original formula:
    ☐ is unchanged   ☐ changes to reflect its new position

11. You cannot copy more than 50 cells at a time.
    ☐ True   ☐ False

12. Which formula(s) won't work in Excel?
    ☐ =B4(B3+C12)   ☐ C4-C5   ☐ =D11^(1−B2)

---

70 Training for Finance

PART 2. GENERAL BUSINESS PROBLEMS

Part Two:

A. General business problems

© 1998 Adkins & Matchett

BUILD BUSINESS SPREADSHEETS USING EXCEL

ABOUT THE GENERAL BUSINESS PROBLEMS

Problem Sets 1 – 4

These sets of problems introduce you to the basic formulas, functions, and modeling structures that you need to know to build business models:

Basic model structure and layout
    Assumptions
    Intermediate calculations
    Results

Data analysis

IF and AVERAGE functions

Date math (calculating with dates)

Absolute reference

Growth calculations

BEFORE YOU START PART 2

Now you're going to build models!

Models, not spreadsheets

Now you are going to start building **models**, a word you will hear in business situations.

What is a model?

Business people often refer to models and model-building. A model is a spreadsheet that lets you play "What-If" games. It has inputs and outputs, and you can affect the outputs by changing the inputs.

Example A spreadsheet that lets you predict future sales by changing pricing and sales rate figures is a model.

A spreadsheet that shows you sales data for the last three quarters is not a model. It's simply a collection of data.

You'll work with data analysis in Problem Set 2, but in all the other problems you'll be building models.

Get your hands dirty

About part 2: a collection of problems

What's the best way to become a good modeler? One word: practice. You must "work out" with Excel until you've built modeling muscles and reflexes. There's a certain wordless, intuitive understanding that comes only after you've worked with spreadsheets for some time. The more you practice, the faster this understanding will arrive.

That's why Part 2 is problem-based. You can't learn Excel or modeling from reading a book. You've got to get your hands dirty solving problems and implementing your solutions.

HOW PART 2 IS STRUCTURED

Each set of problems introduces several specific modeling and Excel skills that you should master.

1.	**Do it together**	Explains the new features and how to use them. Steps you through the solution and its construction.
2.	**You do it**	A similar problem for you to try on your own. May give you some hints.
3.	**Challenge**	A more challenging problem. May offer some new insights or features. May give you some hints.

© 1998 Adkins & Matchett

BUILD BUSINESS SPREADSHEETS USING EXCEL

Get all the practice you can!

If you've just finished Part 1

Do ALL the problems in each problem set. Right now, you need experience and practice, and the more you can get, the better your understanding of models will be. So work your way through all the problems in each set.

If the Challenge problems are too hard, skip them. Go all the way through Sets 1-6 without doing the Challenge problems, then come back and start over again. Do the Challenge problems on your second trip through the material. As I said, there's no substitute for practice.

If you're experienced

Check the list of features at the beginning of each problem set. If you know the material, you might skip the problem set, or go straight to the challenge problem (the last problem in the set) and get some practice.

About the problems

The problems themselves are short and somewhat artificial. For instance, a problem may ask you to compare three investments, whereas on the job you might compare 10, or 100. Or you'll be asked to project a forecast three years, when in real life it would almost always be 5 years or more.

That's deliberate – it's so you can focus on the skill involved and master it. If you do your formulas right, copying your projection out to cover 5, 7, or 10 years is a snap.

The answers and the importance of WHAT-IF

The answers are in the answer section in the back of the book. Be sure to check structure as well as the number answers. Remember, when you're developing a business spreadsheet, **how** you get the answers is almost as important as the answers themselves.

Why? Because in a business model, the initial answer is often just the beginning. Most business people want to ask, "What if we changed something?" "What would happen to profits if we could reduce costs by just one percent?" "What will happen if we reduce prices by 10%? 15%?"

Part 2 will show you how to construct a model which satisfies the business requirement for "What-If" flexibility.

BEST PRACTICES

74 Training for Finance

PART 2. GENERAL BUSINESS PROBLEMS

Build with A B C D

A-B-C-D

You'll learn an A B C D method of spreadsheet construction:

A Analyze
- Analyze the problem
- Figure out the steps needed to get to the solution
- Lay out the assumptions

B Build
- Build the model section by section
- Fill in labels, data and assumptions
- Construct the formulas

C Check
- Check for Excel errors
- Check your construction
- Check your reasoning and logic
- Play "What-If" games and make sure they work

D Document, Decorate, Deliver
- Document your work
- Decorate with number and text formatting
- Deliver a readable, user-friendly printout and file

BUILD BUSINESS SPREADSHEETS USING EXCEL

These settings help you fly!

Change Excel's settings to maximize accuracy and efficiency

Make the following changes. (Not all choices are listed; I'm showing you only the crucial settings. Later, as you're more familiar with Excel, you may decide to change some of these settings. For now, use the set below.)

Go to Tools Options

View menu. Make sure you have these options checked:

- ☑ Formula bar
- ☑ Status bar
- ☑ Comment / Note indicator
- ☑ Gridlines
- ☑ Row & Column Headers
- ☑ Zero Values
- ☑ Horizontal Scroll Bar
- ☑ Vertical Scroll Bar
- ☑ Sheet Tabs

Do NOT check the following option:

- ☐ Formulas

Calculation menu. Use these settings:

- ☑ Automatic calculation — ON
- ☐ Iteration — OFF

Edit menu. Use these settings:

- ☐ Edit Directly in Cell — OFF
- ☐ Fixed Decimal — OFF

Transition menu. Use these settings:

- ☑ Microsoft Excel menus — ON
- ☐ Transition Navigation Keys — OFF

General menu *(non-Excel 97 versions only)*. Make sure this setting is correct:

- ☑ A1 — ON

If you are experiencing problems with Excel's behavior, check these settings.

Optional settings

Make your own decisions about some other settings. I'll show you two settings I prefer. You may like the other options. Make your own choices.

Edit menu

- ☐ Move Selection After Enter — OFF
  Stops the pointer from moving down, up, or sideways after you press Enter.

- ☐ Enable Autocomplete for Cell Values — OFF
  Stops Excel from trying to read your mind and do the typing for you. I don't like a software program trying to second-guess me! It's wrong too often.

PART 2. GENERAL BUSINESS PROBLEMS

SET 1 — BASIC MODELS

Model construction features
- Analyze inputs and outputs before you start building.
- Spell out all calculations
- Calculate a discount
- Trace formulas to check construction
- What-if: Change assumptions to check logic and construction

Excel features
- Trace formulas with special double-click

DO iT TOGETHER — **JET PURCHASE**

THE PROBLEM

Don is negotiating to buy a jet for his company. The aircraft he wants costs $10,500,000. The aircraft company has offered a 7 1/2% discount. It will knock off an additional $600,000 after the discount if Don's company takes responsibility for the final interior fittings and additional instrumentation package. Don has found an outfitter who will do the job for $460,000.

Don must arrive at the final discounted price.

Discussion

This problem is fairly simple. Even so, you should follow good construction practices:

- Separate assumptions (inputs) from results (outputs).
- Show all calculations.
- Make sure your model can answer "What-If" questions like *What happens to the price if we can negotiate a higher discount?*

A is for **Analyze**

Use A – B – C – D to construct your model

Use this simple problem to develop your analysis skills. You'll need them more the more complex your models become.

What is this model's bottom line?

Answer   The final discounted price of the jet

© 1998 Adkins & Matchett

BUILD BUSINESS SPREADSHEETS USING EXCEL

A is for Analyze

What intermediate results do you need to calculate to find the end result?

Answer The amount of the standard discount
The sale price after the discount
The net savings from adding the interior fittings after the sale

What are the assumptions?

Assumption	Value
List price	$10,500,000
Discount	7.5%
Discount for purchase without fittings	_____
Estimated cost of fittings	_____

B is for Build

1. Type the labels and assumption values

Go to Excel and type the labels and assumptions for Don's model. You need to show the intermediate results, so type labels for them as well as for the end result.

Hint: Use the space bar to indent subtotals.

	A	B
1	Don's discount model	
2	**Assumptions**	
3	Standard price	10,500,000.0
4	Discount percentage	7.5%
5	Discount for purchase without fittings	600,000.0
6	Outsourced cost of fittings	460,000.0
7		
8	**Final sale price**	
9	Amount of discount	
10	Sale price with discount	
11	Net savings on fittings	
12	Final sale price	

2. Save the model as **JET**.

3. Construct the formulas.

   a. Start with the amount of the discount.

      Formula for calculating the amount of a discount:

      Multiply the sale price by the discount percentage

9	Amount of discount	787,500.0	=B3 * B4

   b. Calculate the first subtotal: Sale price with discount

10	Sale price with discount	9,712,500.0	=B3 - B9

Training for Finance

c. Calculate the net savings on the interior fittings.

   Savings = difference between the company's fittings discount and the outfitter's price

d.   Calculate the net savings on the interior fittings.

Savings = difference between the company's fittings discount and the outfitter's price

| 11 | Net savings on fittings | 140,000.0 | =B5 - B6 |

e. Calculate the final result: the sale price after all adjustments have been made.

| 12 | Final sale price | 9,572,500.0 | =B10 - B11 |

Step 3. The results

	A	B
1	Don's discount model	
2	**Assumptions**	
3	Standard price	10,500,000.0
4	Discount percentage	7.5%
5	Discount for purchase without fittings	600,000.0
6	Outsourced cost of fittings	460,000.0
7		
8	**Final sale price**	
9	Amount of discount	787,500.0
10	Sale price with discount	9,712,500.0
11	Net savings on fittings	140,000.0
12	Final sale price	9,572,500.0

Great! But you're not through yet, even if you get the same numbers — you **have to** check your work!

C is for Check

To check properly, adjust your Excel settings

1. Go to **Tools Options View** and make sure you can view these features:

   ■ **Formula bar**
   ■ **Status bar**

2. Go to **Tools Options Edit** and uncheck this feature:

   ■ **Edit directly in cell**

If you've already changed this setting, ignore the above!

BUILD BUSINESS SPREADSHEETS USING EXCEL

C is for Check

Check your construction

Look for Excel errors

1. Do you have any error messages like **#REF!**, **#DIV/0!**, or **#VALUE!**? If you do, rebuild the bad formula correctly.

2. Does the Status Bar show the word **Circular** followed by a cell address? If it does, you have a circular reasoning error. *(See Appendix E.)* Check all your formulas and rebuild any that don't match the examples above.

3. Check your formula construction:

You can use Excel's basic formula-tracing technique:

- Go to **Tools Options Edit**
- Make sure **Edit Directly in Cell** is turned off.
- Put your mouse pointer on the formula you want to trace.
- Double-click the mouse.

You'll see the cells that the formula is using.

Or you can put your pointer on the topmost formula and check it by reading the formula in the **Edit Bar**.

C is for Check

Check flexibility and reasoning

Check your model's flexibility and reasoning

Your model can look fine and give you the right answer for the assumptions, but that won't do you much good if the model can't respond to a change in your assumptions or if you used the wrong formulas.

The amateur's error: hard numbers in formulas

The worst error you can make in a business model is to use hard numbers in your formulas instead of assumptions. If you use hard numbers, your model won't change if you change the assumptions, because the assumptions aren't working – they're just sitting there looking pretty. They have to be connected to the formulas to make your model powerful.

No – NO – *NO!*

No – no – NO!

Hard number in formula

8	Final sale price	
9	Amount of discount	=B3 * 7.5%

This kind of formula will KILL your model! Now you can't play what-if games, and you'll look stupid to anyone who knows what a model is supposed to do.

Yes

Correct formula

8	Final sale price	
9	Amount of discount	=B3 * B4

80 Training for Finance

PART 2. GENERAL BUSINESS PROBLEMS

KEY KNOWLEDGE

No hard numbers in output formulas!

No hard numbers in output formulas

Now your model will stand up to changes in the assumptions.

If your model doesn't change when you change your assumptions, you probably have a hard number in a formula.

Examine your formula cells. Put your pointer on each cell and look at the formula in the edit bar

- Do any formulas contain a hard number? There should be NO hard numbers in either formula. Use cell references to the assumptions instead.

Play "What-if" games

Now for the fun part.

Go to your assumptions. Change the percentage from 7.5% to 10%.
- Do your outputs change?
- Do the changes make sense? Your discount should now be $1,050,000.

An easy check

An easy check is to change your assumptions to numbers that will give you a predictable result.

Change all your assumptions except the standard price of the jet to 0. The final sale price should be the same as the standard price, since all the discounts are canceled by the 0s.

- If your model gives a different answer, check your formula construction and your logic.
- If everything checks out, your model is probably all right.
- If you had errors, correct them and save the model again.

Document
Decorate
Deliver

Document

- Are your labels clear?
- Have you shown each step in your derivation of the answer?

Decorate

Format the discount. *(See Appendix D for help.)*
   Percent with two decimals.

Format all other numbers.
   Currency with zero decimals and dollar sign next to the number.

© 1998 Adkins & Matchett

BUILD BUSINESS SPREADSHEETS USING EXCEL

Widen the columns appropriately.

Widen Columns A and B. *(See Appendix D for help.)*

Deliver

Save the model again.

Print the model showing:

- Gridlines
- Row and column headings
- A footer showing the date and time at the right margin *(see Appendix F for details)*

The final result

	A	B
1	Don's discount model	
2	**Assumptions**	
3	Standard price	10,500,000.0
4	Discount percentage	7.5%
5	Discount for purchase without fittings	600,000.0
6	Outsourced cost of fittings	460,000.0
7		
8	**Final sale price**	
9	Amount of discount	787,500.0
10	Sale price with discount	9,712,500.0
11	Net savings on fittings	140,000.0
12	Final sale price	9,572,500.0

Training for Finance

PART 2. GENERAL BUSINESS PROBLEMS

YOU DO IT — ROBERT'S SAVINGS PROGRAM, 1

THE PROBLEM
Robert wants to start a regular savings program. His annual after-tax income totals $34,500. Robert plans to save 5% of that amount. Show Robert's weekly savings and the amount he will save each year. (Assume 52 weeks per year.)

What if...
How much will his savings per month be if he saves 8% per month? (Each month equals 1/12 of the yearly amount.)

A is for Analyze

Analyze
1. What are the end results this model should produce?
   _____
   _____

2. What calculations do you need to make?
   _____
   _____

3. List the assumptions:

Assumption	Value
_____	_____
_____	_____
_____	_____
_____	_____

B is for Build

Enter labels and assumptions
Construct the formulas

1. Type the labels and assumption values

2. Construct the formulas

Reminder: no hard numbers in formulas!

3. Save the model as **ROBERT**.

© 1998 Adkins & Matchett

BUILD BUSINESS SPREADSHEETS USING EXCEL

C is for Check

Checklist

Your model should NOT have:

- ☒ Excel error messages
- ☒ Circular references
- ☒ Hard numbers in formulas

Your model SHOULD:

- ☑ Respond to changes in its assumptions
- ☑ Make sense even if the assumptions change

Document Decorate Deliver

Checklist

- ☑ Show appropriate numbers with percent and dollar formats
- ☑ Print with a header showing your name, the date, and the name of the file. *(See Appendix F for information on printing.)*
- ☒ Do not show a footer
- ☒ Do not print gridlines or row and column headings

YOUR RESULTS

Original assumptions

☐	Weekly savings
☐	Total savings

What if...

Robert saves by the month and changes his savings percentage to 8%?

☐	Weekly savings
☐	Total savings

84 Training for Finance

PART 2. GENERAL BUSINESS PROBLEMS

CHALLENGE — ROBERT'S SAVINGS PROGRAM, 2

THE PROBLEM

After setting up a savings plan (Problem 1), Robert wants to budget his living expenses to see if he can set aside more money for a state-of-the-art audio system.

Robert's expenses and income:

Salary per month	$2,875.00
Fixed expenses per month	$2,050.00
Variable expenses as % of total salary	20%

Robert wants to save anything he doesn't spend on expenses.

Find out how much Robert can save per month. Calculate the percentage of monthly income Robert will devote to savings.

What if...
Robert cuts his basic expenses to $2000 and his incidental expenses to 18% of salary?

Hints

Now you have to deal with months instead of weeks.

Do NOT generate a circular reference in this model! Show total savings in the output area.

(If you don't have a circular reference problem in your construction, then ignore this hint! For more information on circular references, see Appendix H.)

YOUR RESULTS

Original assumptions

[ ]   Savings per month

[ ]   Savings % of salary

What if...

Robert cuts his basic expenses to $2000 and his incidental expenses to 18% of salary?

[ ]   Savings per month

[ ]   Savings % of salary

© 1998 Adkins & Matchett

PART 2. GENERAL BUSINESS PROBLEMS

SET 2 — DATA ANALYSIS

Model construction features
- Separate results and data

Excel features
- Series fill
- Copy formulas
- **IF** function
- **AVERAGE** function
- Sort data

DO IT TOGETHER — SALES PERFORMANCE

THE PROBLEM

You have sales data on four salespeople. You need to summarize the data for the third quarter, show who met their sales goal and who didn't, and calculate average performance per month for each salesperson.

Your boss wants to see a simple YES - NO statement about goal attainment for each person.

The sales data:

	Jul	Aug	Sep	Goal
Bethany	450	400	470	1250
Curtis	300	400	530	1200
Andrew	400	350	375	1250
Dorothea	210	370	410	1000

Dorothea is a new hire and has a lower goal. Curtis is new, too. He has just passed his initial training period and his goal has been raised.

Discussion

Assumptions

This problem contains only one assumption: the sales goal for each salesperson. Should you put it in its own assumption block? In this case, no.

You are massaging data in this problem. Put the goal in the array of data along with everything else.

© 1998 Adkins & Matchett

BUILD BUSINESS SPREADSHEETS USING EXCEL

A is for Analyze

The YES - NO statement
To get the YES - NO statement, you're going to use one of the most powerful functions available: the IF statement. You'll find many uses for IF throughout your career as a modeler.

Averaging
You could use a formula to do the averaging, but you should use a special function for averaging.

1. **What results does this problem need to produce?**

   For each salesperson:
   - Total sales per quarter
   - A *Yes/No* answer to the question: *Did this person meet the sales goal?*
   - An average sales per month figure

2. **What calculations do you need to get to the end results?**

   No secondary calculations are needed – you can go right from data to results.

3. **What about assumptions?**

   There's only one assumption: the quarterly sales goal for each salesperson.

   Place it with the rest of the data.

B is for Build

1. **Set up the quarterly report and its supporting data.**

   In this spreadsheet, separate data from results. The data are monthly; the report is quarterly. The monthly data support the quarterly report. Put the supporting data below it.

	A	B	C	D	E
1	Sales performance				
2					
3	3rd quarter sales performance				
4	Salesperson	Total sales	Goal	Met goal?	Avg. sales/mo.
5					
6					
7					
8					
9					
10	Quarterly performance data				
11	Quarterly	Jul	Aug	Sep	
12	Bethany	450	400	470	
13	Curtis	300	400	530	
14	Andrew	400	350	375	
15	Dorothea	210	370	410	

Training for Finance

2. *Sort the data alphabetically.*

   You could sort by hand as you input the data, but why not have Excel do the work for you?

   > **SORT**
   >
   > **Identify the table**
   >
   > Place the pointer somewhere in the middle of the table. Excel can recognize a table if it doesn't contain any empty rows or columns. If you want more precise control, highlight the table. Just make sure you include all the columns and rows, or you'll sort names without sorting their associated numbers. DISASTER!
   >
   > **Issue the command**
   >
   > Go to **Data Sort** and select the column you want to sort by. You can select up to three sorting criteria and can sort from **A - Z** (ascending) or from **Z - A** (descending).
   >
   > **TIP** Check out the **Options** for date sorting criteria.
   >
   > Your spreadsheet should look like Rows 10 - 15, below.

3. *Build the labels. You can copy the salesperson labels to the results area.*

   It's all right to repeat key information in your results area.

   Enter the goals for each salesperson. Curtis and Dorothea are new hires and have lower sales goals.

   Insert rows if you need more space.

	A	B	C	D	E
1	3rd quarter sales performance				
2					
3	3rd quarter sales performance				
4	Salesperson	Total sales	Goal	Met goal?	Avg. sales/mo.
5	Andrew		1250		
6	Bethany		1250		
7	Curtis		1200		
8	Dorothea		1000		
9					
10	Monthly performance data				
11	Salesperson	Jul	Aug	Sep	
12	Andrew	400	350	375	
13	Bethany	450	400	470	
14	Curtis	300	400	530	
15	Dorothea	210	370	410	

   Layout for the sales performance analysis

BUILD BUSINESS SPREADSHEETS USING EXCEL

B is for Build
BEST PRACTICES

4. **Create a copyable SUM function for Andrew. Copy it down.**

    B5   =SUM(B12:D12)

    ALT =   to get the **SUM** function

    Select **B12:D12**

5. **Create an IF statement for Andrew. Copy it down.**

    =IF(total sales>=goal, "Met", "Not Met")

The IF function

=IF(statement, response if true, response if false)

D5   =IF(B5>=C5,"Met","Not met")

Notice that you can use word responses if you put them in quotes.
Use the   >=   operation sign for "greater than or equal to."
See Appendix B for more information about =IF( ).

If your IF function doesn't work
- Did you forget the two commas? They must be present. They separate the three arguments.
- Did you forget to put quote marks around your words?
- Did you put a comma inside the quote marks? They go outside.
- Do you have the right number of parentheses?

6. **Create an AVERAGE function. Copy it down.**

    Use the Function Wizard or type **=AVERAGE(** to start the function.
    Then click and drag the cells you want to average.
    Check Appendix B for more information on **=AVERAGE**.

    AVERAGE   E5   =AVERAGE(B12:D12)

    Notice that **AVERAGE** works just like **SUM**. It even uses the same arguments in this example.

    Save as **SALESDATA**.

> The IF Function has three parts:
> IF this is true,
> THEN do this,
> OTHERWISE do that!

C is for Check

Check your construction
- No Excel error messages   #REF!   #VALUE!   #NAME?
- No Circular message on Status bar!
- No hard-number assumptions in formulas!

Check your logic
- Results make sense. Check the results of your formulas. Do they make sense?

90   Training for Finance

Document Decorate Deliver

Get it ready to present

- Leave numbers in the **Normal** format. Sometimes business spreadsheets leave out commas to save room, particularly if they don't show money or very large figures.
- Right justify the column labels and center the IF statement cells.

Save the spreadsheet again.

Make it clear, simple, readable!

	A	B	C	D	E	F
1	3rd quarter sales performance					
2						
3	3rd quarter sales performance					Average
4		Salesperson	Total sales	Goal	Met goal?	sales/month
5		Aaron	1125	1250	NO	375
6		Bethany	1320	1250	YES	440
7		Curtis	1230	1200	YES	410
8		Dorothea	990	1000	NO	330
9						
10	Quarterly performance data					
11		Quarterly	Month 1	Month 2	Month 3	
12		Aaron	400	350	375	
13		Bethany	450	400	470	
14		Curtis	300	400	530	
15		Dorothea	210	370	410	

The final result

BUILD BUSINESS SPREADSHEETS USING EXCEL

YOU DO IT   INVENTORY

THE PROBLEM

Set up an inventory analysis that calculates the number of items remaining in inventory at the end of each day and the average number of items sold, and generates an alert if inventory falls below the restock level. Here are the data:

	Item 1	Item 2	Item 3
Inventory at beginning of day	190	25	450
Units sold	50	3	270
Restock level	80	20	200

What if...
What if 110 of Item 1 are sold?

IF statement hint To make the restock alert stand out, show either the word RESTOCK or nothing. To show nothing, use this argument: ""

YOUR RESULTS

Original assumptions

Which items must be restocked?

❏ Item 1   ❏ Item 2   ❏ Item 3

[   ] What is the average number of items sold?

What if...

What if 110 of Item 1 are sold? Which items must be restocked?

❏ Item 1   ❏ Item 2   ❏ Item 3

[   ] What is the average number of items sold?

Training for Finance

PART 2. GENERAL BUSINESS PROBLEMS

CHALLENGE — STOCK PORTFOLIO

THE PROBLEM

Calculate the performance of 3 stocks. You have the following information:

	Stock 1	Stock 2	Stock 3
No. shares	500	400	100
Purchase price	47.00	64.00	75.00
Today's price	41.00	69.00	72.00

Calculate the following:
- The value of each stock holding today
- The total portfolio value
- An evaluation. Which stocks are winners, which are losing?

What if...
What is the total value of the portfolio if Stock 3's price today is 78.00?

YOUR RESULTS

Original assumptions

[ ]   Total portfolio value

What if...
Stock 3's price today is 78?

[ ]   Total portfolio value

© 1998 Adkins & Matchett

93

PART 2. GENERAL BUSINESS PROBLEMS

SET 3

DATE MATH

Model construction features

- B A S E analysis (changes in accounts over time)

Excel features

- Absolute reference in formulas
- Calculating with date math
- Common business number formatting
- Date formats
- Exponentiation in formulas *(Challenge)*

> **NOTE**
> If you'd like to learn more about depreciation and other accounting concepts, find a good book, like Adkins & Matchett's *Introduction to Accounting for Finance*. (You didn't think we'd recommend someone else's book, did you?)

DO IT TOGETHER   THE DEPRECIATION SCHEDULE

THE PROBLEM

You must calculate 1997's depreciation for several items that were purchased during 1997. To be completely accurate, the depreciation should be proportional to the amount of time the items have been owned. Something bought on March 31, 1997, should have only half the depreciation expense of an item bought October 1, 1996, for example.

Here are the data:

Fiscal year-end: September 30

Data	Purchase date	Purchase price	Yearly depn
Milling equipment	14-Mar-97	500,000	20%
New trucks	2-Jan-97	98,500	25%
Plant	15-Nov-96	2,500,000	10%

Discussion: Date math

Date math lets you calculate the number of days between any two dates.

You can type a whole number into any cell, then format it as a date and you'll get a date. How? Excel assigns the number 1 to January 1, 1900 and adds one day for each whole number.

   1 = January 1, 1900

25569 = January 1, 1970

By assigning a number to each date, Excel can add or subtract dates at will — a great advantage for you!

In this problem, you can use date math to find the number of days between the purchase date and the fiscal year-end. Then you can calculate what percentage of the depreciation applies for that time period.

© 1998 Adkins & Matchett   **95**

BUILD BUSINESS SPREADSHEETS USING EXCEL

Step-by-step model construction

How should you set up this model?
Start by thinking of what you need: the depreciation amount for each fixed asset.

How can you get there?

Calculation 1   number of days between FY end and purchase date

Calculation 2   number of days depreciated / number of days in the year

With these two calculations, you can calculate the amount of depreciation for each fixed asset.

This model relies on two unchanging numbers, or **constants**:

The fiscal year end   September 30, 1997

The number of days in 1997   365

When you have a number that will not change under any circumstances and is the same for each item or account treated in the model, you can use a special feature called **absolute reference** in formulas that refer to the constant.

Build the model

1. In this model, the results are the important part. The details are there to support your results. Put the results first:

	A	B
1	**1997 Depreciation**	
2		1997
3	Milling equipment	
4	Trucks	
5	Plant	

2. Next build the supporting calculations, including the constants. Notice how the constants occupy their own area.

	A	B	C	D	E	F	G
7	*Constants*						
8	Days in year	365					
9	FY end	30-Sep-97					
10							
11		Purchase	Purchase	Yearly	Days de-	Depn days	
12	*Data*	date	price	depn	preciated	/ year	Depn. %
13	Milling equipment	14-Mar-97	500,000	20%	200	55%	11%
14	New trucks	2-Jan-97	98,500	25%	271	74%	19%
15	Plant	15-Nov-96	2,500,000	10%	319	87%	9%

Remember to use A B C D

*A constant is a number that will never, **never** change*

If a cell "remembers" a for‑mat you want to delete, clear the format with ALT e a f! (Edit Clear Format)

Training for Finance

PART 2. GENERAL BUSINESS PROBLEMS

3. Build the formulas.

First find the number of days depreciated. It's a simple subtraction, but with a twist. Try the formula the wrong way first:

    E13   =B9 – B13

Note   If you get a date ("27-Sep-00"), reformat the cell with Normal or Comma format.

This formula is correct for the milling equipment, but it won't copy correctly for the trucks or the plant. Try it and see. Can you figure out why?

Right! The copies no longer refer to the fiscal year end.

Normally, formulas copy *relatively*; the pattern of cell relationships is copied, not exact cell addresses.

Go back to the formula for the milling equipment and prepare to fix it. Right now the formula reads:

    E13   =B9 – B13

B9 is a **relative reference**. When you copy it one row down, B9 will automatically adjust downward one row to become B10.

But you want B9 to stay B9 when you copy the formula.

Make B9 an **absolute reference**. Edit the formula to read **=$B$9 – B13**. The **$** signs make the address absolute. All copies will refer to the fiscal year-end cell.

Shortcut

Edit	**F2**
Move to the B9 cell reference	**Home, right arrow**
Apply $ signs	**F4**
	Enter

Copy the edited formula. This time the copy will work.

Note   In Excel 97 you may need to reformat the copied cells.

More about absolute reference

- You can hand-type the $ signs into the formula.
- You can apply the $ signs with **F4** while you're building the formula.
- You actually need the **$** sign only on the row: **=B$9 – B13**. Tap **F4** more than once while you're editing the formula. You'll get four different combinations of **$** signs.
- A range name will have the same effect as the double dollar signs. See the discussion on range names in Appendix E for reasons why you should use range names sparingly.

KEY KNOWLEDGE

Formulas normally copy as a pattern of cell relationships, not as absolute cell addresses.

BEST PRACTICES

© 1998 Adkins & Matchett

BUILD BUSINESS SPREADSHEETS USING EXCEL

> A number as unchanging as 365 days per year could be written into a formula as a hard number. But why not make your computations crystal clear and put it in its own cell?

4. Calculate the Depreciation Days/Year formula.

   Formula = Days depreciated / No. of days in year

   This formula also will need the absolute reference to be copied correctly.

   This time, apply absolute referencing as you're building the formula.

       F13   =E13/$B$8

   For an extra challenge, decide which has to be absolute, the column address or the row.

   The rest is easy. Calculate the actual depreciation percentage for the year:

       G13   =D13 * F13

   Why doesn't this formula need an absolute reference? Because here you want to copy a pattern, not an absolute cell address.

   Finally, calculate the actual depreciation.

       B3   =C13 * G13

   Copy the formula and you're done.

Check

Try the following common-sense checks:

> *Change the milling equipment's Days Depreciated to 365. The Depreciation % should change from 11% to 20% (the full depreciation amount).*
>
> *Immediately restore your original formula by pressing CTRL Z.*

Check for the other usual errors. See Appendix H for a checklist.

Prepare to present your results

1. Whole numbers, like days depreciated, don't need to show decimal places. Use common financial formatting for the prices and depreciation amounts. See Appendix D for more information.

BEST PRACTICES

Common business formatting

- 0, 1, or 2 decimal places for non-percentage figures
- Commas in the thousands place
- Negative numbers in (parentheses)
- 0's visible as 0's rather than - dashes
- Negative and positive numbers aligned on the decimal point

1,234.0
(1,234.0)
0.0

98 Training for Finance

2. Experiment with different date formats and pick one you like.

    CTRL 1
    Number Category Date

    Select from the **Category** list.

3. Notice that you can use two rows for long column labels. It's better to have two rows than a sprawling, wide column.

YOUR RESULTS

Original assumptions

[ ] Truck depreciation

[ ] Days plant is depreciated in 1997

What if...

Truck's yearly deprecation percentage changes from 25% to 40%?

[ ] Truck depreciation

© 1998 Adkins & Matchett

BUILD BUSINESS SPREADSHEETS USING EXCEL

YOU DO IT — STOCK CHECKER

THE PROBLEM

Create a stock checker that compares today's stock price with the purchase price and tells you whether the stock has gained or lost.

Use the purchase date and today's date to determine how many days each of the stocks has been held.

Show which of the stocks was bought less than 6 months ago and is still subject to the high short-term capital gains tax. (Short-term capital gains tax applies to the profits on any stock held less than 6 months.)

Assume "Today" is May 7, 1998, so you can check your results against the solution.

Stock	PowerCo	RetailHut	BizMag
Today's price / share	$44.50	$125.88	$64.25
Purchase price / share	$42.38	$125.50	$72.13
Purchase date	Mar. 12, 1994	May 5, 1998	Feb. 22, 1995

What if:
What if PowerCo was bought on November 14, 1997 for $41.00?

Save as **CHECKER**.

Hints

Use absolute reference and IF statements to help arrive at a solution.

YOUR RESULTS

Original assumptions

Which stock would be subject to a short-term capital gains tax if sold today?
❑ PowerCo   ❑ RetailHut   ❑ BizMag

Which stocks gained?
❑ PowerCo   ❑ RetailHut   ❑ BizMag

[   ] Days **PowerCo** has been held

What if...

What if PowerCo had been bought on November 14, 1997 for $41.00?

Which stock would be subject to a short-term capital gains tax if sold today?
❑ PowerCo   ❑ RetailHut   ❑ BizMag

[   ] Days **PowerCo** has been held

PART 2. GENERAL BUSINESS PROBLEMS

CHALLENGE — INVESTMENT RETURNS

Special feature: Sophisticated formula writing using exponentiation

This is a tough one! You might skip it if you've never done financial math problems.

THE PROBLEM

The Moores want to compare returns on three very different investments:

	Zero coupon	Painting	Gold
Purchase price	10,000	10,000	12,000
Purchase date	1/1/97	2/1/96	3/1/97
Today's value	10,500	14,000	12,100

Assume that "today" is May 7, 1998.

The Moores have an annual investment return goal of 10% for each investment and for overall portfolio gain.

Carolyn Moore wants to see what each investment's return is today (May 7, 1998). She also wants a quick and easy way of seeing which investments have met their return goal of 10%.

What if:
What if the gold had actually been bought on June 1, 1997?

Hints

Use the following formula to calculate the return:

$$\left(\left(\frac{\text{Future value}}{\text{Present value}}\right)^{\frac{1}{\text{no. of years}}}\right) - 1$$

Future value = Sale price
Present value = Purchase price
Excel uses the ^ symbol to show exponentiation.
Calculate number of periods in days.

Use the Comma format with 0 decimal places for the money values.

Show percentages to 3 decimal places.

Exponents in Excel:
Cell $B4^2$ = B4 ^ 2

© 1998 Adkins & Matchett

BUILD BUSINESS SPREADSHEETS USING EXCEL

YOUR RESULTS

Original assumptions

Which investment(s) met the Moores' performance goal?
- ❏ Zero coupon   ❏ Painting   ❏ Gold

[   ] Average total gain

What if...

What if the gold had actually been bought on June 1, 1997?

Which investment(s) would meet the Moores' performance goal?
- ❏ Zero coupon   ❏ Painting   ❏ Gold

[   ] Average total gain

PART 2. GENERAL BUSINESS PROBLEMS

SET 4 GROWTH CALCULATIONS

Model construction features

- Calculating growth by percentages and by the addition of whole dollar figures
- Structure assumptions when calculating growth over time
- Using *figures in millions*
- Setting up baseline data

Excel features

- Growth formulas
- Series fill
- Text wrapping
- Formula checks

DO IT TOGETHER — SPACE REQUIREMENTS

THE PROBLEM

Project the accounts in this problem. Each account grows at some amount and each requires a different type of modeling solution.

Accounts like these are typical of what you'll see in many budget and financial statement projections.

	A	B	C	D	E
1	**How accounts grow**				
2	figures in millions				
3					
4	*Assumptions*	Constants	Year 1	Year 2	Year 3
5	Sales growth / year		5%	6%	8%
6	Fixed asset growth / year		70	100	125
7	Acquisitions growth in $	10			
8	Depreciation growth / year	5%			
9					
10	*Results*	Baseline year	Year 1	Year 2	Year 3
11	Sales	1,100			
12	Fixed assets	1,400			
13	Acquisitions	500			
14	Depreciation	300			

What if?

Acquisitions grow at $12 million per year and sales growth per year is as follows?

	Year 1	Year 2	Year 3
Sales growth / year	8%	10%	11%

© 1998 Adkins & Matchett

BUILD BUSINESS SPREADSHEETS USING EXCEL

About growth calculations

Growth calculations are an important part of many business models. It's important to set them up and execute them correctly.

Growth formulas

Percentage growth	= Previous unit * (1 + growth factor)
Growth by addition of an amount	= Previous unit + amount of growth

Make your assumptions as flexible as possible!

Try putting constants in a column of their own!

Setting up growth assumptions

If you're calculating growth for several periods, set up your assumptions so that you can use a different growth rate for each period.

In each account, the assumptions drive the growth. Each account's growth is based on an increase over last year's amount. Increases are either set dollar figures or percentages.

1. **Prepare the assumptions.**

   Notice that two of the assumptions are constants and two vary from year to year. Two are percentages and two are dollar amounts.

	A	B	C	D	E
1	How accounts grow				
2	figures in millions				
3					
4	*Assumptions*	Constants	Year 1	Year 2	Year 3
5	Sales growth / year		5%	6%	8%
6	Fixed asset growth / year		70	100	125
7	Acquisitions growth in $	10			
8	Depreciation growth / year	5%			

2. **Input the time period labels.**

   Use Series Fill to help input the year labels.

   Series Fill is a useful feature that will save you a ton of time. Learn it by practicing it. See the next page for details.

104 Training for Finance

PART 2. GENERAL BUSINESS PROBLEMS

SERIES FILL

Type Year 1 and Year 2 in the appropriate cells. Format them as bold centered text.

	C	D
4	Year 1	Year 2

Select both cells. Notice the handle (little box) in the lower right border of the selected cells.

Year 1	Year 2

Hint If you can't see the handle, go to **Tools Options Edit** and make sure **Allow Cell Drag and Drop** is checked.

Click and drag the handle. Drag one cell to the right and you should see:

4	*Assumptions*	Constants	Year 1	Year 2	Year 3

Series Fill lets you create a series of numbers just by dragging. Excel needs to know what series you have in mind, so give it a pattern to follow by inputting the first two numbers in your series.

Excel also recognizes several word sequences, like days of the week and months of the year.

Try the three Series Fills below. Type the inputs in two touching cells, then drag the two cells across or down. Notice how Excel continues the pattern when you use Series Fill.

Qtr 1	Qtr 2

Jan	Feb

5
3

Warning

Series Fill can hurt you, too. If you use mouse drags to copy numbers (a common habit), Excel will occasionally do a Series Fill when you don't expect it. Then you'll end up with wrong numbers that you won't easily notice.

To be safe, I never copy with the drag feature. See Appendix A for safer copying shortcuts.

Keyboard version of Series Fill

Highlight the two "pattern" cells and the empty cells you want to fill. Then use **ALT e i s**. If it doesn't work, you probably need to change settings in the dialog box appropriately.

This is one case where using the mouse is easier.

© 1998 Adkins & Matchett

BUILD BUSINESS SPREADSHEETS USING EXCEL

Baseline year, Base year, Year 0, Historical year

Back to the model!

Finish inputting the labels and the baseline year figures. You'll need those as a starting point for your growth calculations.

The baseline year is a year that has already happened. The baseline year column contains historical information. Years 1, 2, and 3 are projections or forecasts. They haven't happened yet.

	A	B	C	D	E
9					
10	*Results*	Baseline year	Year 1	Year 2	Year 3
11	Sales	1,100			
12	Fixed assets	1,400			
13	Acquisitions	500			
14	Depreciation	300			

Wrapping text

In the example, the words **Baseline year** are too wide for the column. Nobody likes a big sprawling column label! Use one of two solutions:

1) Use two or more rows to type the label. This solution appeared in the Set 3 Challenge.

2) Wrap the words inside the cell (the solution you see in the example).

WRAP TEXT

- Highlight the text you want to wrap.
- **Format Cells Alignment Wrap Text**   *Shortcut: Use CTRL 1*

Note: All the cells in the row expand to maintain the wrapped cell's height.

The growth formulas

Build the sales growth formula. It's percentage growth, so use this formula:

Previous year * (1 + growth rate)

Growth formula, Year 1: **Cell C11:**   = B11 * (1 + C5)

Copy the formula across. Notice how the assumption layout lets you copy the formula accurately.

	A	B	C	D	E
10	*Results*	Baseline year	Year 1	Year 2	Year 3
11	Sales	1,100	1,155	1,224	1,322

The fixed assets account is growing by a dollar amount each year. Use the formula:

Previous year + $ amount of growth

For Year 1, **Cell C12:**   = B12 + C6

106 Training for Finance

PART 2. GENERAL BUSINESS PROBLEMS

	A	B	C	D	E
		Baseline			
10	*Results*	year	Year 1	Year 2	Year 3
11	Sales	1,100	1,155	1,224	1,322
12	Fixed assets	1,400	1,470	1,570	1,695

Results of the Sales and Fixed assets formula

The next two formulas are just like the Sales and Fixed assets growth formulas, except that they use constants instead of a separate assumption for each year. Although constants are not used as often as separate assumptions for each year, you do need to know how to create and copy formulas that use them.

Review Problem Set 3 if you don't know how to create formulas using constants. Don't use range names! See Appendix E for reasons why.

	A	B	C	D	E
1	**How accounts grow**				
2	*figures in millions*				
3					
4	*Assumptions*	Constants	Year 1	Year 2	Year 3
5	Sales growth / year		5%	6%	8%
6	Fixed asset growth / year		70	100	125
7	Acquisitions growth in $	10			
8	Depreciation growth / year	5%			
9					
10	*Results*	Baseline year	Year 1	Year 2	Year 3
11	Sales	1,100	1,155	1,224	1,322
12	Fixed assets	1,400	1,470	1,570	1,695
13	Acquisitions	500	510	520	530
14	Depreciation	300	315	331	347

The solution

The mark of an amateur

Make sure you have not used hard numbers like this:

   B11 * 1.05

Such a practice is the mark of an amateur. Good business formulas must be able to respond to "What-If" changes in the assumptions.

Check your formula by putting 0 in each growth assumption. If you wrote the formulas correctly, your results should be the same in all years.

The double-click advantage

For a graphic picture of the cells in your formulas, try this little-known Excel feature:

Go to **Tools Options Edit** and uncheck **Edit Directly in Cell**. Return.

Put your pointer on one of your formulas and double-click it. The cells that make up the formula will be highlighted.

Use this feature often as a quick and easy formula structure check.

Amateurs!

No – NO – *NO!*

BEST PRACTICES

© 1998 Adkins & Matchett

BUILD BUSINESS SPREADSHEETS USING EXCEL

YOUR RESULTS

Original assumptions

[   ] Year 3 Acquisitions

[   ] Year 3 Sales

What if...

Acquisitions grow at $12 million per year and sales growth per year rises as follows?

	Year 1	Year 2	Year 3
Sales growth / year	8%	10%	11%

[   ] Year 3 Acquisitions

[   ] Year 3 Sales

PART 2. GENERAL BUSINESS PROBLEMS

YOU DO IT — SPACE REQUIREMENTS

THE PROBLEM

You must project your company's personnel space requirements for the next 3 years.

- Each employee requires 140 square feet of space.
- Currently the company employs 32 people.
- The company is renting 4480 square feet of space with an option to expand into unused space on the same floor.
- You know that the company is planning to expand its personnel by the following percentages:

	Year 1	Year 2	Year 3
Personnel growth	30%	20%	20%

What if...
What if personnel growth is actually	50%	30%	10%?

Hints

Use Series Fill to help input the year labels.

The formula for space requirements uses a constant for the amount of space each person needs. Since you don't expect this number to change from year to year, you don't need to put it in all three years. But you do need to show it; someone might want to expand or reduce it at a later date.

You could skip the personnel calculation and simply apply a growth formula to the space requirement. You'd get the same answer. But normally people want to see the drivers, or figures that drive the model. In this case, that driver is the number of people hired.

The model is clearer when the people calculation is included.

Save as **SPACE**.

Drivers: numbers that make the model change

© 1998 Adkins & Matchett

BUILD BUSINESS SPREADSHEETS USING EXCEL

CHALLENGE — INVESTMENT RETURNS

THE PROBLEM

Maria owns The Calculator Hut on New Street, behind the New York Stock Exchange. She is having a one-day sale on three of her most popular calculators. On the sale day she is selling them at a 25% reduction from the regular retail price.

	Calc 1	Calc 2	Calc 3
Cost	$0.99	$2.44	$14.25
Markup percentage	500%	450%	300%

Calculate the following for each calculator:
- The regular retail price
- The one-day retail sale price

Also calculate averages for the cost, markup percentage, regular price, and sale price.

What if:
What if Maria raises her sale discount to 30% and also raises her markups as follows?

	Calc 1	Calc 2	Calc 3
Markup percentage	550%	500%	400%

Hints

Calculate the sale price with a negative growth formula.

If you copy the **AVERAGE** function down the column, the format will copy too. Consider using the **Edit Paste Special Formula** command to copy the formula without its format. Check Appendix E for more information on this useful command.

YOUR RESULTS

Original assumptions

☐ Average markup

☐ Sale price, Calc. 3

What if...

What if the sale discount is 30% and the markups go up as follows?

	Calc 1	Calc 2	Calc 3
Markup percentage	500%	450%	300%

☐ Average markup

☐ Sale price, Calc. 3

KEY KNOWLEDGE

Edit Paste Special lets you paste part of a cell's information: formats, formulas, values, and more

Part Two:

B. Financial math problems using Excel functions

BUILD BUSINESS SPREADSHEETS USING EXCEL

ABOUT THE FINANCIAL MATH PROBLEMS

Problem Sets 5 and 6

Problem Sets 5 and 6 introduce you to calculations using Excel's basic financial math functions:

PV   **FV**
NPV   **IRR**

In addition, the sets include a mention of **RATE** and **PMT**.

The problems include:

PV	Car payments
	Compare 3 investments
	Bullet payment
	Delayed payments
FV	Savings plan
	Single deposit
NPV	Present value of new factory
	Compare 3 investments
IRR	Return on new factory
	Compare 3 investments
RATE	Find the interest rate on a loan
PMT	Find the amount of a car payment

I am assuming that you already know basic financial math and concepts like present value and future value. If you don't, you can treat the problems as pure Excel problems and discover how to make the functions work properly.

For a good grounding in basic financial math and time value of money concepts, see Adkins & Matchett's *Introduction to Financial Math using the HP 17B / 19B Calculators*.

SET 5

PART 2. FINANCIAL MATH PROBLEMS

PV AND FV

Model construction features
- Indent column
- Time consistency in financial functions

Excel features
- PV and FV financial functions
- Optional arguments in functions

DO IT TOGETHER — EMMA; ROBERT, AGAIN

THE PROBLEMS

Problem 1. Emma's car payments
Emma borrowed $24,659 and made a hefty down payment when she bought her new car. She is financing the car by paying $500 a month on a 5-year loan at an interest rate of 8%. What is the present value of her payments? How much does she actually pay?

What if:
What if Emma paid $500 per month at 9.5% interest?

Problem 2. Robert's savings plan
Robert plans to save $50 a week for 5 years. His savings account pays 5 1/2% compounded weekly. (Assume a 52-week year.)

What will Robert's savings, compounded weekly, be worth after 5 years?

What if:
What if Robert saves $60 a week at an interest rate of 5.625%?

Discussion

The danger point in using most financial functions is your treatment of time. Make sure your time units are consistent. If your payments are monthly and interest is expressed yearly, you must use a monthly interest rate or you'll get the wrong answer.

Set up your assumptions and results labels just as in any other model.

Save as **GROWTH**.

WARNING

© 1998 Adkins & Matchett 113

BUILD BUSINESS SPREADSHEETS USING EXCEL

Emma's car payments

Hints

1. Make Column A very narrow. This trick helps you indent. Notice how the example below indents everything below the section headings, which are in Column A.

2. Look at Rows 1 and 10 in the illustration below. They are wider than normal. Widening a row is an option you can use to separate one section from another. Try it: drag the lower row boundary with your mouse.

	A	B	C
1		Present value of Emma's car payments	
2		*Assumptions*	
3		Monthly payment	$500.00
4		Interest rate/year	8.00%
5		Life of loan in years	5
6		No. of periods/year	12
7		*Present value*	
8		Total amount paid	
9		PV of payments	
10		Robert's savings planner	
11		*Assumptions*	
12		Weekly savings	$50.00
13		Number of savings periods per year	52
14		Number of years of savings	5
15		Interest rate on savings	5.50%
16		*Savings program*	
17		Total amount saved	
18		Future value of savings	

Setup for the two problems

Build the formulas

1. The first one's easy.

    Total amount paid on the loan: **C8**   =C3 * C5 * C6

2. Now for the present value. The formula for present value is complicated, so Excel offers you a function that will do the calculation for you. As in all functions, you simply fill in the arguments correctly and the function will do the rest. Here is an example of a function and its arguments.

A typical function

IF Function   =IF(statement, response if true, response if false)

Code for formulas and functions. Tells Excel to calculate what follows

Name of function. Tells Excel which to pick from the list of functions

Arguments in parentheses give the function the info it needs to calculate

Functions can make your life easier IF you use them correctly!

PART 2. FINANCIAL MATH PROBLEMS

The PV function

When to use the PV function

The PV function will work for this problem because the payments are regular and don't change from beginning to end of the cash flow stream. If you are trying to calculate present value for a stream of cash flows that is irregular or with varying sizes, you can't use this function. See Problem Set 6 for the solution to these kinds of problems.

$$=PV(rate, nper, pmt, fv, type)$$

The **bolded** arguments are necessary, the *italicized* arguments are optional.

rate   The interest rate or discount rate

nper   The number of periods

pmt   The regular payment. Excel usually expects you to input a payment as a negative number.

fv   A single future cash flow which will be added to the payment in the final period. You'll learn how to use this option in the Challenge problem in this set.

type   0 = payments are due at the end of the period *(default option)*.
           1 = payments due at the beginning of the period.

*Use PV **only** when the cash flows are even!*

The time problem

Time units must be consistent. In this problem, the interest rate is annual, the payments are monthly. You must do some work to make sure the time units are right.

- You must translate annual interest into monthly interest;
- You must make sure the number of periods is correct.

You might be tempted to use hard numbers in the problem. After all, the year is not going to suddenly change from 12 months to 10 months. But put your time units in your assumptions so that you can change your time units easily.

PV function   C9   =PV(C4/C6, C5*C6, –C3)

If your answer is negative, you forgot to make the payment negative.

	A	B	C
7		**Present value**	
8		Total amount paid	$30,000.00
9		PV of payments	$24,659.22

PV compared to actual dollars paid

© 1998 Adkins & Matchett 115

Problem 2. Robert's savings program

The description and setup are on Pages 113 – 114.

Build the formulas

The first one's easy.

Total amount saved: **C17**   =C12 * C13 * C14

For the future value calculation, you could use a complicated formula, but Excel offers the FV function which will do the work for you. It's almost exactly like the PV function.

Like PV, the FV function works only if the payments are regular and unchanging in size.

$$=FV(\textbf{rate},\textbf{nper},\textbf{pmt},\textit{pv},\textit{type})$$

The bold arguments are necessary, the italicized arguments are optional.

rate   The interest rate

nper   The number of periods

pmt   The regular payment. Excel usually expects you to input a payment as a negative number.

pv   A single value that occurs at time 0 and will be added to the calculation of future value. You'll learn how to use this option in the Challenge problem in this set.

type   0 = payments are due at the end of the period *(default option)*.
1 = payments due at the beginning of the period.

Remember, Robert's payments are monthly, so the rate and number of periods must be input in monthly terms, too.

FV function   **C18**   =FV(C15/C13, C13*C14,–C12)

If your answer is negative, you forgot to make the payment negative.

It's all about time

A	B	C
16	*Savings program*	
17	Total amount saved	$13,000.00
18	Future value of savings	$14,954.22

FV of savings compare to total dollars placed in savings account

Check

Change Robert's savings program to a monthly program, saving $216.67 a month. Don't forget to change the number of periods per year, too.

You should get about the same answer.

PART 2. FINANCIAL MATH PROBLEMS

Deliver *(see Appendix D for more information)*

Show two decimal places and currency format for the money values.

Show 0 decimal places for non-currency figures.

Show two decimal places for the percentages.

YOUR RESULTS

Original assumptions

[   ] Present value of Emma's payments

[   ] Future value of Robert's savings

What if...

What if Emma's interest rate were 9.5%?

[   ] Present value of Emma's payments

What if Robert were able to save $60 per week at 5.625% interest?

[   ]. Future value of Robert's savings

BUILD BUSINESS SPREADSHEETS USING EXCEL

> This problem uses financial math term, *discount rate*. Think of it as *interest rate*.

YOU DO IT — COMPARE THREE ANNUITIES

THE PROBLEM

You can use PV to compare the present values of different investments. In this problem, set up a model that will let you compare three annuities. Each one pays out a set amount to you once a year (at the end of the year).

The discount rate is 8% for all three, and each costs $10,000.

	Annuity 1	Annuity 2	Annuity 3
Life in years	5	3	6
Annual payment	$2,700	$4,500	$2,250

What if:
What if Annuity 1 paid you $3,375 each year for 4 years? Would it be worth more than the original Annuity 1 offer?

Analysis

Each annuity pays out exactly the same amount of money, but over different periods. Which one should you buy? The present value function will answer the question.

Calculate the actual amount of money paid out by each annuity as well as the present value of each.

Which annuity offers you the most value (has the highest present value)?

Build

> When in doubt, go for flexibility in your assumptions!

Since the discount rate is the same for all investments, you may be tempted to make it a single constant. Don't! Under some circumstances, the discount rate can be different for different investments. Leave your options open and show the discount rate for each annuity.

Save as **PVCOMP**.

YOUR RESULTS

Original assumptions

The most attractive annuity is: ❏ No. 1   ❏ No. 2   ❏ No. 3

[   ] PV of best annuity

What if...

What if Annuity 1 offered payments of $3,375 for 4 years?

[   ] PV of new Annuity 1 offer

118 Training for Finance

PART 2. FINANCIAL MATH PROBLEMS

CHALLENGE — BULLETS & SINGLE DEPOSITS

Single payments at the end of a loan's life are called bullet payments!

THE PROBLEM

Problem 1. Your cousin wants you to lend him $3,500. He says he'll pay you back $5,000 in one lump sum after 5 years. You could invest the $3,500 at a return of 8% (the "discount rate"). Is the loan a better deal for you?

What if:
What's your opinion of the deal if the discount rate is 7%?

Problem 2. Your aunt tells you she is depositing $5,000 into a 5.5% savings account for you. The savings account compounds daily. How much will the account be worth at the end of 10 years, when she will turn it over to you?

What if:
What if the compounding is monthly rather than daily?

Hint

Even though PV and FV are set up to calculate the value of steady streams of regular cash flows, you can use them to calculate a single amount if you turn to the optional arguments.

Tip for the bullet payment problem

You know that there are no payments between now and the bullet payment, therefore payments are 0. You know what the value of the payment will be in the future ($5,000). Use the optional *fv* argument to find the PV of the bullet payment.

Tip for the single deposit problem

Work it out! It's the same as the bullet payment problem, except that you know what the present value is and the payment is 0.

© 1998 Adkins & Matchett **119**

BUILD BUSINESS SPREADSHEETS USING EXCEL

YOUR RESULTS

Original assumptions

☐ Present value of the bullet payment at 8%

☐ Future value of the single deposit

What if...

The loan discount rate is 7%?

☐ Present value of the bullet payment

The single deposit compounding is monthly?

☐ Future value of the single deposit

PART 2. FINANCIAL MATH PROBLEMS

SET 6

NPV AND IRR

Model construction features

- Show figures in thousands

Excel features

- NPV and IRR financial functions
- Using Function Wizard to learn strange functions
- Getting help about functions

DO IT TOGETHER — FACTORY PURCHASE

THE PROBLEM

Generica Corp. is going to purchase a new factory for $5,000,000. The company has estimated the cash flows that the factory will generate during its operation:

Year 1	$1,500,000
Year 2	$2,000,000
Year 3	$3,000,000

The discount rate is 12%.

You must determine the net present value of those cash flows and the internal rate of return of the investment.

What if:
What if the discount rate is 14%?

What if the discount rate is 12% and the initial cost is $4,500,000?

If you don't know financial math, you might want to skip this section! It doesn't cover any other significant material.

Curious about financial math? You could try our Introduction to Financial Math workbook.

Discussion

1. You can't use **PV** to solve this problem because the cash flows are *uneven* — different in each year. But you can use a function called **NPV**. And the **IRR** function will give you a rate of return.

2. You're dealing with big numbers here. Do what many businesses do: show figures in thousands or millions. You just type the numbers as thousands and note that you've done so in some prominent place on the worksheet. Look at the setup below for an example.

   This practice works fine as long as you are consistent and you remember that you've "sized" all the money amounts on your model.

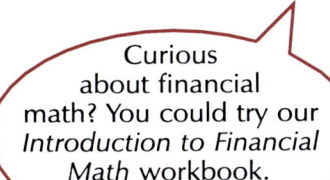

© 1998 Adkins & Matchett 121

BUILD BUSINESS SPREADSHEETS USING EXCEL

Set up your assumptions and results labels just as in any other model.

	A	B	C
1		**Return on new factory**	
2		*figures in thousands*	
3		***Cash flows***	
4		D.R.	12.000%
5		Price	($5,000.00)
6		Cash flow, Year 1	$1,500.00
7		Cash flow, Year 2	$2,000.00
8		Cash flow, Year 3	$3,000.00
9		***Return***	
10		NPV	
11		Net present value	
12		IRR	

Setup for the problem

Hints

1. Set up Column A as a very narrow column for indenting.

2. Notice how the *figures for thousands* reminder is set up.

The NPV function

When to use the NPV function

Use **NPV** when payments are **not** regular ("uneven stream of cash flows"). IF your cash flows are completely even, use the **PV** function.

$$=NPV(\text{discount rate}, \text{cashflow}_1 : \text{cashflow}_n)$$

discount rate   The discount or interest rate

cash flows   The cash flows. Enter either a range or a list of cells.

What about the number of periods?

You can see the NPV function lets you input the rate and the cash flows. What about the number of periods? NPV finds the number of periods from counting the cells in the cash flow argument.

Note   Use a zero for any period that does not have a cash flow. A blank cell will give you a wrong answer. Here's an example:

Cash flows	
Year 1	$0.00
Year 2	$400.00
Year 3	$700.00

YES

blank cell →

Cash flows	
Year 1	
Year 2	$400.00
Year 3	$700.00

NO

WARNING

122 Training for Finance

PART 2. FINANCIAL MATH PROBLEMS

The two things you must know about NPV

1) The **NPV** function is called the "net present value" function. But it doesn't really give you **net** present value. You must subtract the cost of the investment from the **NPV** answer to get true net present value.

2) IMPORTANT! Don't include the initial cost in the cash flow range! You'll get the wrong answer.

Does NPV mean net present value? What do you do with the initial cost?

Build the formulas

1. Set up the **NPV** function in Cell **C10**.

    =NPV(d.r.,cash flows)

    =NPV(C4,C6:C8)

    Don't...

    Don't include the cost of the factory!

2. Calculate the true net present value in Cell **C11**:

    C11   =C5 + C10

    or   =SUM(C5,C10)

The IRR function

The IRR function is built like the NPV function, with one big and one little difference. *And* the cash flows must be entered as a range, not a list.

Excel 5, 7:   IRR   =IRR(*guess*,cashflow$_0$:cashflow$_n$)

Excel 97:   IRR   =IRR(cashflow$_0$:cashflow$_n$,*guess*)

IRR! Like NPV, but with an important difference! Initial cashflow is included!

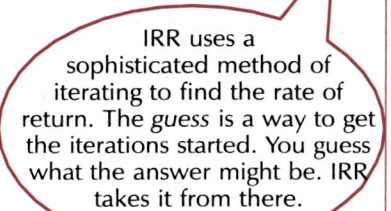

The big difference

You **must** include the initial cost in the cash flows! The **IRR** function must contain at least one negative number (initial cost) or it won't work. Try it!

The little difference

You don't have to enter a discount rate for most **IRR** problems. Notice that the argument is optional. The **IRR** function works out the rate for itself and usually doesn't need to be "jump-started" with a guess.

IRR uses a sophisticated method of iterating to find the rate of return. The guess is a way to get the iterations started. You guess what the answer might be. IRR takes it from there.

Weird behavior of the IRR

When you have a stream of cash flows that make more than one change from positive to negative, you may get more than one answer to the IRR problem. However, most of those solutions are nonsense numbers and will look completely wrong. In other words, you will have to rely on your common sense to evaluate the answers.

If an answer looks completely wrong, check over your formula construction first. Then try changing the guess.

© 1998 Adkins & Matchett

More about the guess

If your IRR function returns an error and there are no mistakes in your formula construction (in particular, you've included at least one negative number in your cash flow stream), try putting in a guess to jumpstart the IRR calculation from a different position. The default guess is 10%. Try a very large number, like 2, or a very small number, like 0.001%.

Now build the IRR function in the model. Notice that after all this talk about the guess being optional, you're going to refer to the discount rate anyway. It'll help with the checking.

Excel 5, 7   C12   =IRR(C4,C5:C8)
Excel 97   C12   =IRR(C5:C8,C4)

	A	B	C
9	*Return*		
10		NPV	$5,069.01
11		Net present value	$69.01
12		IRR	12.71%

The final results

Check

Here's an interesting way to check your calculations. If the internal rate of return is exactly the same as the discount rate, the net present value will be 0.

Check by copying the IRR result *as a value* into the discount rate cell. If you've set up the model correctly, net present value should fall to 0.

> Use Edit Paste Special to copy formulas as values

Hint

Copy the 12.71% internal rate of return with **CTRL C**.

Move to Cell **C4**.

Use **Edit Paste Special Value** to paste the exact value of the IRR result, 0.127147484413839.

Once you've confirmed that net present value falls to 0, use **CTRL Z** to undo your copy and return to the original discount rate. Hit **ESC** to clear out the clipboard.

> Find out more about Edit Paste Special in Appendix E!

Present

Format all percentages to 3 decimal places.

Save as **FACTORY**.

PART 2. FINANCIAL MATH PROBLEMS

YOUR RESULTS

Original assumptions

Does the factory have a positive return?   ❑ Yes   ❑ No

[　　　　　　　] Net present value (initial cost subtracted)

[　　　　　　　] IRR

What if...

The discount rate changes to 14%?

Does the factory have a positive return?   ❑ Yes   ❑ No

[　　　　　　　] Net present value (initial cost subtracted)

[　　　　　　　] IRR

What if...

The discount rate is 12% and the initial cost is $4,500?

Does the factory have a positive return?   ❑ Yes   ❑ No

[　　　　　　　] Net present value (initial cost subtracted)

[　　　　　　　] IRR

© 1998 Adkins & Matchett

BUILD BUSINESS SPREADSHEETS USING EXCEL

YOU DO IT — COMPARE 3 INVESTMENTS

THE PROBLEM

Compare three investments. Each one has an upfront purchase price of $1,000,000. Find their net present values and internal rates of return.

The cash flows (in thousands) and discount rates:

	D. R.	Year 1	Year 2	Year 3	Year 4	Year 5
Oil field	9.5%	250	250	250	300	300
Bond	9.0%	90	90	90	90	1090
Real estate	8.5%	200	200	200	300	600

What if:
What if the oil field's cash flow changed?

	D. R.	Year 1	Year 2	Year 3	Year 4	Year 5
Oil field	9.5%	200	200	300	400	300

What if:
What if the real estate's discount rate were 9.0%?

Save as **NPVCOMP**.

YOUR RESULTS

Original assumptions

What is the net present value (initial cost subtracted) and IRR of each investment?

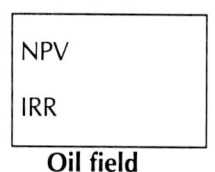

NPV		NPV		NPV
IRR		IRR		IRR
Oil field		**Bond**		**Real estate**

What if...

What is the net present value (initial cost subtracted) and IRR of the revised oil field investment?

NPV
IRR
Oil field

NPV
IRR
Real estate

What if the real estate's discount rate were 9%?

PART 2. FINANCIAL MATH PROBLEMS

CHALLENGE — RATE AND PMT FUNCTIONS

THE PROBLEMS

Use two new functions, **RATE** and **PMT,** to solve certain problems.

Part A You're curious about the payments needed to buy a $38,000 car. What would your monthly payments be if you took out a 5-year loan at 8% interest for the whole amount?

Part B What's the annual interest rate on a 5-year loan of $4,495 if monthly payments are $92?

What if...
What is the car loan payment if you pay a down payment of $7,200?

What if...
What is the annual loan interest rate if the monthly payments are $95 ?

USE PASTE FUNCTION *(EXCEL 97)* / FUNCTION WIZARD

Use *Paste Function* to discover how to use new functions.

Access *Paste Function* with either **Insert Function** or the *Function Wizard* icon. Select a category, then find the function you want to use.

The screens you see are not particularly helpful. Ask for help; you'll find an explanation of the function and usually some examples of how to use it.

Hints

These are simple models. Set them up like any other problem, with input and output sections, ready to answer "What-IF" questions.

Use the Function Wizard's **Help** feature to find out how to use the **RATE** and **PMT** functions.

YOUR RESULTS

Original assumptions

[ ] The car payment

[ ] The *annual* loan interest rate

What if...

[ ] What is the car payment if you make a down payment of $7,200?

[ ] What is the *annual* loan interest rate if the monthly payments are $95?

© 1998 Adkins & Matchett 127

Part Two:

C. Financial statement forecasts

BUILD BUSINESS SPREADSHEETS USING EXCEL

ABOUT THE FORECASTING PROBLEMS

Note You need basic accounting knowledge to fully understand some of the material in this section.

If you need an accounting introduction or review, try Adkins & Matchett's *Introduction to Accounting for Finance*.

The Problem Sets

Problem Sets 7 – 10 introduce two important subjects:

- Projecting financial statements
- Setting up a complex model in a multiple-sheet file

Problem Set 7 Secondary calculations and plug accounts
  Property plant & equipment
  Retained earnings
  Calculating a balance sheet plug account

Problem Set 8 Projecting financial statements on a single sheet
  Assumptions
  Secondary calculations
  Income statement
  Balance sheet
  Cash flow statement
  What-if scenarios

Problem Set 9 Introduction to multiple sheets
  Budget
  Oil field analysis
  What-if scenarios

Problem Set 10 Projecting financial statements on multiple sheets
  Assumptions
  Secondary calculations
  Income statement
  Balance sheet
  Cash flow statement
  What-if scenarios

Additional helpful material

Problem Sets 1 - 2 Analysis, structuring, and checking tools
Problem Set 3 B A S E analysis, absolute reference in formulas
Problem Set 4 Growth formulas

SET 7

PART 2. FINANCIAL PROJECTIONS

PROJECTION PREP

Model construction features
- BASE analysis
- Supporting calculations for financial projections
- Calculation of a "plug" number
- Use of negative numbers in a forecast

Excel features
- Circular reasoning errors
- Using SUM functions inside another formula

DO IT TOGETHER — FIXED ASSET ANALYSIS

THE PROBLEM

You need to project a company's use of property, plant and equipment over a period of 3 years. Here's the data:

Future growth assumptions

	Historical year	Year 1	Year 2	Year 3
Growth in new purchases		5%	10%	10%
Sales of equipment % of new purch.		5%	5%	5%

Historical year information

New purchases	300.0
Sales of old equipment	12.0
Gross fixed assets, ending	4,000.0

What if:
What if Growth in new purchases falls to 6% in Years 2 and 3, and Sales of equipment rises to 10% in Year 3?

What is a projection?

A projection tries to foresee the future financial performance of a business unit, company, or individual. The projections you'll make in these exercises are standard "base case" projections. They assume that the future will continue to look like the past.

For example, if you are projecting your personal budget for next year, you will probably assume that your food costs will continue to be about the same as they were last year. They probably won't double or be cut in half.

© 1998 Adkins & Matchett

You need two sets of information to make a projection:

Historical info Information about past performance. Usually projections show 3 – 5 years of historical information. You'll work with only one historical year in these exercises.

Assumptions Estimations of future performance. The most common types of assumptions are:

Growth An account will increase by a certain percentage. Sales assumptions are usually growth assumptions.

Percentage Percentage of another account. For instance, costs are usually projected as a percentage of sales. If sales goes up, so will costs. Sales is the *driver* for many other accounts in a projection.

Dollar amounts This kind of assumption is not as common as percentage assumptions, but it does appear sometimes for some accounts like the repayment of loans.

Sales **drives** most other accounts in a projection

B A S E analysis and plug accounts

When you project a set of financial statements, you will often need to project complex accounts by separating individual increases and decreases in the account. You may also need to calculate a "plug" number to balance one side of the balance sheet.

You'll perform both tasks in this set, helping you prepare for a full-sized financial statement projection in the next set of problems.

B A S E analysis

You can use **B A S E** analysis to calculate the change in an account over time. Your challenge is to set up the model so that you can project the account accurately with one set of copyable formulas.

B	Amount at beginning of year
A	+ Any additions during the year
S	− Any subtractions during the year
E	= Ending amount

B A S E analysis

Build

Set up the assumptions and the historical year data.

PART 2. FINANCIAL PROJECTIONS

	A	B	C	D	E	F
1		Plant, property and equipment (PP&E)				
2		figures in millions	Historical	Projected		
3			Year 0	Year 1	Year 2	Year 3
4		*Assumptions*				
5		Growth in new purchases		5%	10%	10%
6		PP&E sales % of new purch.		5%	5%	5%
7						
8		*Projection*				
9		Gross PP&E, beginning				
10		New purchases	300.0			
11		Sales of old equipment	12.0			
12		Gross PP&E, ending	4,000.0			

Setup for the PP&E problem

Your job: create copyable formulas

Keep in mind that you should create copyable formulas in Year 1. You should be able to copy Year 1's formulas across to all other years.

Apply this to the **B A S E** analysis. Row 9 is the **B** part of the **B A S E** analysis: the beginning amount. What copyable formulas go here?

Remember that the beginning of any fiscal year (FY) is exactly the same as the ending of the previous FY. Use a cell reference in **D9** to the ending of the previous year to get the beginning amount.

    D9 =C12

	A	B	C	D
9		Gross PP&E, beginning		4,000.0
10		New purchases	300.0	
11		Sales of old equipment	12.0	
12		Gross PP&E, ending	4,000.0	

=C12

Setting up the Beginning amount formula

Create a growth formula for New purchases in Year 1:

    D10 =C10 * (1 + D5)

Create a percentage formula for the sales of old equipment in Year 1.

    D11 =D10 * D6

Classic B A S E analysis!

Use the **B A S E** formula to calculate the ending amount.

    PP&E, beginning amount
    + New purchases
    − Sales of old equipment
    PP&E, ending amount

    D12 =D9 + D10 − D11

© 1998 Adkins & Matchett

Now you have copyable formulas for all cells. Copy them across to complete your projection.

	A	B	C	D	E	F
1		Plant, property and equipment (PP&E)				
2		figures in millions	**Historical**	**Projected**		
3			Year 0	Year 1	Year 2	Year 3
4		*Assumptions*				
5		Growth in new purchases		5%	10%	10%
6		PP&E sales % of new purch.		5%	5%	5%
7						
8		*Projection*				
9		Gross PP&E, beginning		4,000.0	4,299.3	4,628.4
10		New purchases	300.0	315.0	346.5	381.2
11		Sales of old equipment	12.0	15.8	17.3	19.1
12		Gross PP&E, ending	4,000.0	4,299.3	4,628.4	4,990.5

Results of the projection

Positive and negative numbers in projections

In this example, you left all numbers positive and subtracted the negative numbers in the formulas.

You could also make the number for sales of old equipment negative, then use a **SUM** function to get the ending amount.

Mathematically, either way works. Check your company's preferences, or look at the annual report to see how they handle the issue. Nowadays, many companies don't normally show expenses as negatives on their projections.

Make your own choices on this issue.

YOUR RESULTS

Original assumptions

☐ New purchases, Year 3

☐ Gross fixed assets, ending balance Year 3

What if...

What if Growth in new purchases falls to 6% in Years 2 and 3 and Sales of equipment rises to 10% in Year 3?

☐ New purchases, Year 3

☐ PP&E, ending balance Year 3

PART 2. FINANCIAL PROJECTIONS

YOU DO IT — RETAINED EARNINGS

THE PROBLEM

Use B A S E analysis to calculate retained earnings. Set the problem up the same way you set up the PP&E analysis.

Projection assumptions

	Historical year	Year 1	Year 2	Year 3
Net income		85.0	93.0	100.0
Dividends % of net income		25%	25%	25%

Historical year information

Retained earnings, beginning	
Net income	80.0
Dividends	20.0
Retained earnings, ending	500.0

What if:
What if dividends were 40% of net income in all three projected years?

Save as **RETAINED**.

YOUR RESULTS

Original assumptions

[   ] Retained earnings at the end of Year 3

What if...

What if dividends were 40% of net income in all 3 projected years?

[   ] Retained earnings at the end of Year 3

© 1998 Adkins & Matchett

BUILD BUSINESS SPREADSHEETS USING EXCEL

Plugging a "leaky" balance sheet!

Assets must always = Liabs. & Equity

CHALLENGE — PLUG ACCOUNTS

When you project a balance sheet, the projected years often don't balance – an unacceptable condition! As a last resort, modelers sometimes create a ***plug account*** whose only purpose is to balance the balance sheet. Usually it's Cash that becomes the plug.

You will create a plug account in this problem.

THE PROBLEM

Set up the following balance sheet projection. So you can focus on the plug, the other accounts are simple hard numbers, and Liabilities and equity have been combined into one account.

	A	B	C	D	E	F
1	Plug account					
2		*figures in millions*				
3			Base Year	Year 1	Year 2	Year 3
4	**Assets**					
5		Cash	65.0			
6		Current assets	45.0	50.0	60.0	70.0
7		Fixed assets	150.0	200.0	250.0	300.0
8		Total assets	260.0			
9						
10	**Liabilities and Equity**					
11		L&E	260.0	325.0	380.0	435.0

Setup for the plug account

Your job is to calculate Cash as a plug so that the balance sheet balances. You must create the formula without creating a circular reference.

What-If
What if Current Assets are 85 in Year 3?

Analysis

Create a **SUM** function to add the assets. Caution! Add ALL the assets. Include the empty Cash cell.

3			Base Year	Year 1	Year 2	Year 3
4	**Assets**					
5		Cash	65			
6		Current assets	45	50.0	60.0	70.0
7		Fixed assets	150	200.0	250.0	300.0
8		Total assets	260	250.0	310.0	370.0
9						
10	**Liabilities and Equity**					
11		L&E	260	325.0	380.0	435.0

Assets and L&E do not balance!

The Balance sheet doesn't balance. It has more L&E than Assets. Therefore, it need more assets to balance. The Cash formula has to calculate the difference between L&E and Assets.

PART 2. FINANCIAL PROJECTIONS

$$\begin{array}{r}\text{Liabilities \& Equity}\\ -\quad\underline{\text{Assets}}\\ \text{Cash}\end{array}$$

Formula for the Cash plug

The CIRCULAR REFERENCE problem

Be careful! Your first instinct may get you in trouble.

You may be tempted to use this formula:

   D5   =D11 – D8

If you do, you will get a *circular reference*. See Appendix H for a full discussion of circular references.

Use double-clicking to trace the formula. It's circular because it refers to itself. The Total assets formula includes Cash; Cash is calculated using the Total assets formula.

WARNING

Reminder
Tools Options Edit
Turn **Edit Directly in Cell** off.

Excel settings for the double-click feature

Notice that when you have a circular reference, you can see a Circular notice on the Status Bar. The notice appears on every open worksheet even if the circular reference is in another spreadsheet.

Circular references are unacceptable unless you are deliberately using them to solve problems that cannot be solved any other way.

And if you have heard something about using iterations to "cure" circularities, don't! Not unless you understand iterations completely, know what the use of iterations does to your spreadsheet and how to fix the horrible problems that the use of iterations can generate.

Create the formula without a circular reference. Add the individual asset accounts.

   D5   =D11 – SUM(D6:D7)

SUM within another formula

Notice that you can use **SUM** within another function or formula. You can't use the **ALT =** shortcut or the **SUM** icon when you're in the middle of a formula. Just type **SUM(** and select the cells like you always do.

Save this model as **PLUG**. You can use it as a reference later, when you're building an entire financial projection.

© 1998 Adkins & Matchett

BUILD BUSINESS SPREADSHEETS USING EXCEL

YOUR RESULTS

Original inputs

[   ] Cash plug, Year 3

Does the Balance Sheet balance?   ❑ Yes   ❑ No

Do you have a circular reference?   ❑ Yes   ❑ No

What if...

Current Assets are 85 in Year 3?

[   ] Cash plug, Year 3

Does the Balance Sheet balance?   ❑ Yes   ❑ No

Do you have a circular reference?   ❑ Yes   ❑ No

PART 2. FINANCIAL PROJECTIONS

SET 8   PROJECTION , ONE SHEET

Model construction features

- Create a full financial statement setup and projection using one sheet
- Project growth and percentage formulas with the help of supporting calculations
- Create a balancing plug for the balance sheet
- Check the model with What-If games

Excel features

- Circular references
- Window Freeze Panes
- Window Split
- Repeat title rows on printout

THE PROBLEM

Project a financial statement for three years. You will work with a set of assumptions and one year of historical information.

Discussion

Organize your model into sections. Assumptions come first because they control everything else.

```
┌─────────────────────┐
│     Assumptions     │
└─────────────────────┘

┌─────────────────────┐
│  Income statement   │
└─────────────────────┘

┌─────────────────────┐
│    Balance sheet    │
└─────────────────────┘

┌─────────────────────┐
│ Cash flow statement │
└─────────────────────┘

┌─────────────────────┐
│      Secondary      │
│    calculations     │
└─────────────────────┘
```
Layout of sections

© 1998 Adkins & Matchett

Use one column for each year. Put all the information relating to that year in that column.

	Hist. year	Year 1	Year 2	Year 3
Assumptions		x%	x%	x%
Income statement	yyyy.y	yyyy.y	yyyy.y	yyyy.y
Balance sheet	zzzz.z	zzzz.z	zzzz.z	zzzz.z
Cash flow statement	aaa.a	aaa.a	aaa.a	aaa.a
Secondary calculations	bbbb.b	bbbb.b	bbbb.b	bbbb.b

Column layout

Set up the assumptions

	A	B	C	D	E	F
1	Financial statement forecast					
2		figures in millions		Historical	Projected	
3				Year 0	Year 1	Year 2	Year 3
4	Assumptions					
5		Income statement				
6		Sales growth			5.0%	6.0%	7.0%
7		COGS % of sales			62.0%	62.0%	62.0%
8		SG&A % of sales			26.0%	26.0%	26.0%
9		Taxes % of Net income before taxes			40.0%	40.0%	40.0%
10	Asset assumptions					
11		Current assets % of sales			21.0%	21.0%	21.0%
12		Investments growth / year			12.0%	12.0%	12.0%
13	Liabilities assumptions					
14		Current liabilities % of sales			18.0%	18.0%	18.0%
15		Long-term debt $ amount			120.0	120.0	120.0
16	Equity assumptions					
17		Capital stock $ amount			420.0	420.0	420.0

Assumptions for the projection

- Notice the layout. The assumptions are divided into sections that match the financial statement sections, and the assumptions in each section follow the order in which the accounts appear on a financial statement.

  Setting up your assumptions this way will make it easier for you — or your client — to find specific assumptions when examining your model.

- Notice how the historical and projected year labels are arranged. The historical year heading is in italics. The "Projected" label is centered over columns D – F. See Appendix D if you don't know how to do this.

- Examine the assumptions. Two are growth formulas. Two are dollar amounts. The rest are percentages of other accounts.

PART 2. FINANCIAL PROJECTIONS

Build the Income statement

First, build the Income statement's labels and historical data.

20	**Income statement**	
21	Sales	650.0
22	COGS	400.0
23	Gross margin	250.0
24		
25	SG&A	169.0
26	Net income before taxes	81.0
27	Taxes	32.0
28	Net income	49.0

Income statement labels and historical information

> Normally, you'd show 3 – 5 years of historicals

Most projections show 3 – 5 years of historical data. To make life easier for you, this forecast will use just one historical year.

The Income statement formulas

Build Year 1, check it, then copy it across to Years 2 and 3.

Year 1 should be all formulas with no hard numbers in them (the 1 in a growth formula doesn't count!) Use these formulas to project the income statement:

Growth	Sales
Percentage of sales	COGS, SG&A
Subtotal	Gross margin, net income before taxes, net income

The example below will get you started.

20	**Income statement**			
21	Sales	650.0	=C21 * (1 + D6)	Growth
22	COGS	400.0	=D21 * D7	Percentage
23	Gross margin	250.0	=D21 - D22	Subtotal

First three formulas in the Income statement

Now finish the Income statement on your own.

19	**Income statement**				
20	Sales	650.0	682.5	723.5	774.1
21	COGS	400.0	423.2	448.5	479.9
22	Gross margin	250.0	259.4	274.9	294.2
23					
24	SG&A	169.0	177.5	188.1	201.3
25	Net income before taxes	81.0	81.9	86.8	92.9
26	Taxes	32.0	32.8	34.7	37.2
27	Net income	49.0	49.1	52.1	55.7

The completed Income statement

© 1998 Adkins & Matchett

BUILD BUSINESS SPREADSHEETS USING EXCEL

Build the Balance sheet

Enter the Balance sheet labels and historical information. Start in Row 29.

29	Balance sheet	
30	Assets	
31	Cash	407.0
32	Current assets	136.5
33	Investments	353.0
34	**Total assets**	**896.5**
35		
36	Liabilities	
37	Current liabilities	116.5
38	Long-term debt	120.0
39	Equity	
40	Stock and APIC	420.0
41	Retained earnings	240.0
42	Total equity	660.0
43	**Total liabilities and equity**	**896.5**

Balance sheet labels and historical information

Some tricks for working with a large sheet!

Splitting and freezing the screen

As you work down the sheet, at some point the year headings and the assumptions will disappear from the top of the sheet. It would be nice to still see them, or to see both the assumptions and the balance sheet at the same time.

Excel offers two options for dealing with this situation.

FREEZE PANES

Windows Freeze Panes — "Freezes" either rows, columns or both in a frame at the top left of the window.

Try it — Put your pointer in Cell **A4**, then **ALT w f**. Move down the page. Notice that the rows above your cell pointer's original position are now "frozen" in place and are visible no matter how far down the sheet you go.

CTRL Home and you'll go to **A4**, the new "Home" position.

To remove **Window Freeze Panes**, simply give the **ALT w f** command again from any point on the sheet.

PART 2. FINANCIAL PROJECTIONS

> *It's either - or! You can't use Freeze and Split together*

WINDOW SPLIT

Turn off Window Freeze Panes if it's on.

Window Split	Splits your window into two windows. You can see two separate parts of the same sheet.
🖱	Look for the little bar that sits right on top of the vertical scroll strip. Grab it with your mouse. Drag it down slowly and release it somewhere around the middle of the screen.
Remove split	Drag the bar back up with your mouse.
Vertical split	Find the little bar to the right of the horizontal scroll strip and drag it.
F6	Use F6 to jump back and forth across the bar.

Split the window so that you can see the assumptions in the top window and the Balance sheet in the bottom window. Now you can build your formulas without scrolling. Use **F6** to jump back and forth from window to window.

Balance sheet formulas

Cash	*Leave this formula till later!*
Current assets	Percentage of sales
Investments	Growth
Total assets	Subtotal *(include cash)*
Current liabilities	Percentage of sales
Long-term debt	Cell reference to assumption line
Stock and APIC	Cell reference to assumption line
Retained earnings	*Leave this formula till later!*
Total equity	Subtotal *(include retained earnings)*
Total liabilities and equity	Subtotal

What about Retained earnings?

The Retained earnings account has to be calculated separately. Normally, modelers show separate (or **supporting** or **secondary**) calculations in a separate area, since they're not part of most financial statements.

Yes, I know you could cram the Retained earnings calculation into one cell, but good modeling practice requires that you split out complex calculations into steps, for two reasons:

1. *It documents what you've done.* Other people know exactly how you've calculated the accounts.

2. It's much, much *easier to proofread and revise* a model that shows its secondary calculations in detail! Save yourself future pain and set it up right.

Yes, this particular calculation is almost too simple to put in a separate area. But in a more complex model, your Retained earnings calculation would be more complex. Do this step just for the practice of setting up and using a calculations area.

© 1998 Adkins & Matchett

Set up a Calculations area

Go to Row 62 and set up the *Retained earnings* calculation. Since it's not part of the output but is just a secondary calculation, it should go in some out-of-the-way spot like the bottom of the sheet.

62	Calculations	
63	Retained earnings calculations	
64	Retained earnings at beg. of year	
65	Net income	49.0
66	Retained earnings at end of year	240.0

Calculations area for Retained earnings

Use **BASE** analysis to project Retained earnings. It's easy because there's no S (for subtraction). Then use a cell reference to connect your result to the *Retained earnings* account in the balance sheet

Complete all of the Balance sheet except the *Cash* account.

BASE analysis again!

29	Balance sheet				
30	Assets				
31	Cash	407.0			
32	Current assets	136.5	143.3	151.9	162.6
33	Investments	353.0	395.4	442.8	495.9
34	**Total assets**	**896.5**	**538.7**	**594.7**	**658.5**
35					
36	Liabilities				
37	Current liabilities	116.5	122.9	130.2	139.3
38	Long-term debt	120.0	120.0	120.0	120.0
39	Equity				
40	Stock and APIC	420.0	420.0	420.0	420.0
41	Retained earnings	240.0	289.1	341.2	397.0
42	Total equity	660.0	709.1	761.2	817.0
43	**Total liabilities and equity**	**896.5**	**952.0**	**1,011.4**	**1,076.3**

Assets don't equal Liabilities & Equity!

It's an accounting rule! A = L&E

Create the Cash plug

Notice that in each projected year, assets are less than liabilities & equity.

An unacceptable condition! You must make sure the Balance sheet balances.

In this projection, you'll make *Cash* a plug account to do the balancing automatically. Since this forecast is short on Assets as compared to Liabilities & equity, *Cash* is an ideal account to serve as a balancing plug number.

Make sure you don't create a circular reference.

      D31   =Total L&E – SUM(all asset accounts except Cash)

Review Problem Set 7 for details on how to construct the plug properly.

PART 2. FINANCIAL PROJECTIONS

Build the Cash flow statement

Set up the Cash flow statement labels. This set of labels will work in just about any Cash flow statement, with appropriate additions or deletions. But it's hard to get historical information to fit into this generic form, so don't put historical numbers in your Cash flow statement.

In real life, you might put in historical subtotals and a few key accounts like Net income, Capital expenditures, Depreciation and Dividends. But trying to fill in the details might cause you problems, since annual reports often change account categories from year to year and historical data won't balance in your generic form.

> *Remember, this is a greatly simplified model for practice purposes!*

45	Cash flow statement	
46	Net income	
47	(Inc.)/dec. in operating assets	
48	Inc./(dec.) in op. liabilities	
49	Cash flow from operations	
50		
51	(Inc.)/dec. in investments	
52	Cash flow from investing activities	
53		
54	Inc./(dec.) in debt	
55	Inc./(dec.) in capital stock	
56	Cash flow from financing activities	
57		
58	Net change in cash	
59		
60	Balance Sheet change in cash	

The Cash flow statement labels

> *Net income represents the change in Retained earnings*

Notice that each account on the Balance sheet is represented on the Cash flow statement, either directly or indirectly. Which account on the Balance sheet does Net income represent?

Notice how the labels show you whether the account should be positive or negative. The easiest way to construct the cash flow statement is to show the impact on cash for each account. Then you can simply subtotal the three categories and not have to worry about signs in the SUM function.

If this discussion sounds like something in a foreign language to you, you need to learn more about cash flow statements. Try a book like Adkins & Matchett's *Introduction to Accounting for Finance*.

Build the Cash flow statement formulas

Each formula (except for Net income) measures the change in an account from previous year to current year. The only difficult part about building these formulas is making sure you get the signs right. Here's a key:

If an increase is positive   Subtract previous year from current year
If an increase is negative   Subtract current year from previous year

© 1998 Adkins & Matchett

Here are the formulas for the *Cash flow from operations* section:

Net income	D46	=D27
(Inc.)/dec. in operating assets	D47	=C32 − D32
Inc./(dec.) in op. liabilities	D48	=D37 − C37
Cash flow from operations	D49	=SUM(C46:C48)

44	A	B	C	D	E	F
45		Cash flow statement				
46		Net income		49.1	52.1	55.7
47		(Inc.)/dec. in operating assets		(6.8)	(8.6)	(10.6)
48		Inc./(dec.) in op. liabilities		6.3	7.4	9.1
49		Cash flow from operations		48.7	50.9	54.2

Cash flow from operations

Using the operations section as a guide, complete the *Cash flow from investments* and *Cash flow from financing* sections.

50	A	B	C	D	E	F
51		(Inc.)/dec. in investments		(42.4)	(47.4)	(53.1)
52		Cash flow from investments		(42.4)	(47.4)	(53.1)
53						
54		Inc./(dec.) in debt		0.0	0.0	0.0
55		Inc./(dec.) in capital stock		0.0	0.0	0.0
56		Cash flow from financing activities		0.0	0.0	0.0

Cash flow from investments and from financing

Now sum up all three sections to get the Net change in cash.

| 58 | | Net change in cash | | 6.3 | =SUM(D49,D52,D56 |

Formula for the Net change in cash

If you haven't made a SUM function that adds up non-touching cells, look at Appendix B for info on how to do so.

How do you know you're right?

After all this work, how do you know you did the Cash flow statement correctly? Check it against the Balance sheet! The change in cash as calculated from the Balance sheet should be the same as the Net change in cash shown on the Cash flow statement.

Add this line to your cash flow statement:

59					
60		Balance Sheet change in cash		6.3	=D31 - C31

The balance sheet check

> The formula: This year's cash from the B/S
> − <u>Previous year's cash from the B/S</u>
>   Balance sheet change in cash

If your B/S check equals your Net change in cash, your Cash flow statement is correct.

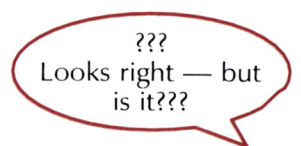

??? Looks right — but is it???

PART 2. FINANCIAL PROJECTIONS

Checklist

❏ No circular references

❏ No Excel error messages like **#REF!** or **#VALUE!**

❏ Cash flow statement foots with balance sheet (Line 58 = Line 60)

❏ Balance sheet balances

❏ Accounts look reasonable. Scan from left to right across each account. Do any accounts rise or fall sharply in the first projected year? There may be an error somewhere.

❏ No hard numbers in input formulas!

Here's the fun part! This is why people build models!

CHECK YOUR RESULTS WITH *WHAT-IF* GAMES

Check your results by putting your model to work. Do what your client would do: change assumptions and watch the model respond.

Arrange your screen with **Window Split** so that you can see the assumptions and the Net income line at the same time.

Original assumptions

[   ]   Net income, Year 3

What-If no. 1

The company wants to increase its profits. What will happen if it increases Sales growth?

	Year 1	Year 2	Year 3
Sales growth	8.0%	12.0%	12.0%

Your results

[   ]   Net income, Year 3

❏ Yes ❏ No Does the Balance sheet still balance?

❏ Yes ❏ No Does the Cash flow statement still foot with the Balance sheet?

❏ Yes ❏ No Do the different assumption changes produce changes in the accounts?

❏ Yes ❏ No Do the changes make sense? (If Sales goes up, does Net income go up?)

© 1998 Adkins & Matchett

BUILD BUSINESS SPREADSHEETS USING EXCEL

What-If no. 2

IMPORTANT! First change the Sales growth assumptions back to their original values:

	Year 1	Year 2	Year 3
Sales growth	5.0%	6.0%	7.0%

What if the company cuts costs?

	Year 1	Year 2	Year 3
COGS	60.0%	60.0%	60.0%
SG&A	25.0%	25.0%	25.0%

Your results

[   ] Net income, Year 3

❑ Yes ❑ No Does the Balance sheet still balance?

❑ Yes ❑ No Does the Cash flow statement still foot with the Balance sheet?

❑ Yes ❑ No Do the different assumption changes produce changes in the accounts?

❑ Yes ❑ No Do the changes make sense? (If Sales goes up, does Net income go up?)

Try changing other assumptions. Every change should produce an appropriate result in other accounts.

Deliver

Set up the model for printing.

- Create a footer. Show the following *(Check Appendix F for how-to info)*:
  Page numbers
  The name of the model
  The date and time
  Your name

- Show Rows 1 - 3 on each printed sheet.
  Don't copy the rows down the page! Go to the **File Setup Sheet** command. Click in the **Rows to Repeat at Top** box. Then click anywhere in Row 1 and drag through Row 3. Release and **Enter**.

Print the model and admire your work!

148 Training for Finance

PART 2. FINANCIAL PROJECTIONS

SET 9

MULTIPLE SHEETS

Model construction features
- Building a model using multiple sheets
- Totals and Constants column

Excel features
- Cross-sheet formulas: how to read them, how to create them
- Renaming sheets

DO IT TOGETHER   BUDGET

Here's more practice to get you ready for financial statement projections!

THE PROBLEM

You must project your department's budget for 3 years, based on the following information:

	Base year	Year 1	Year 2	Year 3
Assumptions				
Inflation rate		3%	4%	5%
Benefits % of salaries		37%	37%	37%
Square feet of office space		2,200.0	2,200.0	2,200.0
Cost per square foot		120.0	120.0	120.0
Base year data				
Salaries	360,000.0			
Benefits	133,200.0			
Cost of office space	264,000.0			

What-if
See the Results section for **What-If** games.

Discussion

You already know how to build a model like this one. The formulas are nothing new if you've gone through the other problem sets. What's different about this problem? It uses more than one sheet.

© 1998 Adkins & Matchett   **149**

Many models are built across more than one sheet. It's convenient to place one section on one sheet. Flipping from sheet to sheet is easier than scrolling down a long page.

Guidelines for dividing a model onto separate sheets

- Put each major section on a separate sheet.
- If your model doesn't divide neatly into sections, put one printed page on each sheet.

The budget problem has two sections: assumptions and the budget itself. You'll put each one on a separate sheet.

| Sheet1 | Assumptions |
| Sheet2 | Budget |

About multiple-sheet models

Tip   Here's the most important point you should remember when you set up a multiple-sheet model:

- Keep your columns consistent! For example: put Year 1 in the same column on all sheets!

Set up your sheets

1. Rename one sheet **Assumptions** and the next sheet **Budget**.
2. Group both sheets.

GROUP SHEETS

Group sheets in bunches
Click on first sheet tab. Hold down **SHIFT.** Click on last sheet tab.

Group individual sheets
Click on first sheet tab. Hold down **CTRL.** Click on another sheet tab. Keep clicking until you've selected all the sheets you need.

Group all sheets
Click the right mouse button on a sheet tab. Select **Select All Sheets.**

Ungroup sheets
Move to an ungrouped sheet
   or
Click the right mouse button on a sheet tab. Select **Ungroup Sheets.**

How do you know sheets are grouped?
1) Look at the top band of the window, where you see the filename. If the sheets are grouped, you will see **[Group]** after the filename.
2) Look at the sheet tabs. Grouped sheet tabs are lighter in color than ungrouped sheet tabs.

WARNING! *Read this!*
Be very careful when you work with grouped sheets. Don't forget to ungroup them! Anything you do to the first grouped sheet happens to all the grouped sheets. You could ruin your entire model....

PART 2. FINANCIAL PROJECTIONS

Move to the *Assumptions* sheet. Hold down **CTRL** and click on the *Budget* sheet tab.

Notice the name bar at the top of the page. Now it says **[Group]**, and both sheet tabs are white. These two signals tell you you have grouped some sheets.

Be careful! Now anything you do to *Assumptions* will also occur on *Budget*.

Enter the title and the column headings. Adjust column widths.

	A	B	C	D	E	F
1	Budget					
2			*Base*	*Projected*		
3			*Year*	Year 1	Year 2	Year 3

Working with grouped sheets

Important! Exit Group mode now! Click on an ungrouped sheet, or use the sheet tab mouse menu. You don't want to keep entering on both sheets at once.

3. Set up your assumptions on the **Assumptions** sheet. Be sure you leave the Base Year column empty!

> Leave the Base Year column in place, even if there's nothing in it on this sheet!

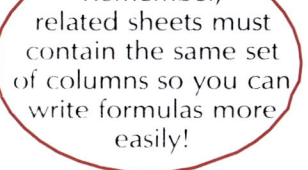

	A	B	C	D	E	F
1	Budget					
2			Base	Projected		
3	Assumptions		Year	Year 1	Year 2	Year 3
4		Inflation rate		3%	4%	5%
5		Benefits % of salaries		37%	37%	37%
6		Square feet of office space		2,200.0	2,200.0	2,200.0
7		Cost per square foot		120.0	120.0	120.0

Set up the Assumptions sheet

> Remember, related sheets must contain the same set of columns so you can write formulas more easily!

4. Move to the Budget sheet.

NAVIGATE THROUGH SHEETS

Click on sheet tab.
Click scroll buttons to the left of the sheet tabs.

CTRL Page Down and **CTRL Page Up**

© 1998 Adkins & Matchett

BUILD BUSINESS SPREADSHEETS USING EXCEL

5. Set up the budget labels and base year data on the Budget sheet.

	A	B	C
1	Budget		
2			Base
3		Budget projection	Year
4		Salaries	360,000.0
5		Benefits	133,200.0
6		Cost of office space	264,000.0
7		Total	757,200.0

Set up the Budget sheet

Build the formulas

It might help you to see both sheets at once. You can't use **Window Split** with multiple sheets. You have another option, though.

ARRANGE WINDOWS TO SEE SEVERAL SHEETS

You can create two windows and see two or more sheets at once. Use **Window New Window Arrange Horizontal**.

Create a new window
1. Close any other spreadsheets that are open.
2. Window New Window
   Stop and check:
      Do you see :2 at the end of the filename? You should.
      Open the **Window** menu. Do you see two versions of your current file listed as open? You should.

Arrange the windows
   Window New Window Arrange Horizontal

Work with the windows
   Jump from window to window with **CTRL F6**

Close the additional window

   Click the **Close** button at the upper left corner of one of the windows.

   Maximize the remaining window. (Click the Maximize button in the upper right corner of the window.)

Arrange the Assumptions and Budget windows so you can see both of them at once.

Notice how neatly the columns line up on both sheets. Everything about Year 1 is in Column D no matter which sheet you're on.

152 Training for Finance

PART 2. FINANCIAL PROJECTIONS

1. Build the projection formulas. Start on the Budget sheet. You'll have to go to the Assumptions sheet to pick up the assumption cell. Easy!

BUILD CROSS-SHEET FORMULAS

Build a cross-sheet formula just like any other formula!

1. Start in the cell where the result should appear.

    Use your mouse! Click on the first cell in the formula. If it's on another sheet, click on the sheet tab or use **CTRL Page Up** or **Down** to move to the other sheet, then click on the cell.

2. Enter an operation sign.
3. Click on the next cell.
4. When you've clicked on the last cell, **Enter**.

How to read a cross-sheet formula

='Assumptions'!D8   *Cell D8 on the Assumptions sheet*

- sheet name
- cell address
- separator. Separates sheet name from cell address.

Examples   =D4*'IncState'!D21   *Cell D4 on this sheet * Cell D21 on the IncState sheet*

Build the *Salaries* formula.

Salaries are inflating at 3% per year. Inflation calls for a growth formula.

Budget D4   Base year salaries * (1 + salary growth assumption)

How-to	Step by step
1. Start in cell where you want the result.	*Budget* sheet, Cell **D4**
2. Start the formula.	=
3. Click on the first cell.	Click **C4**
4. Type an operation sign.	* (1 +
5. Click the next cell.	Move to *Assumptions*. Click **D4**
6. **Enter** after you've clicked the last cell.	Enter

© 1998 Adkins & Matchett   **153**

BUILD BUSINESS SPREADSHEETS USING EXCEL

Finish the model

	A	B	C	D	E	F
1	Budget					
2			*Base*	*Projected*		
3	*Budget projection*		Year	Year 1	Year 2	Year 3
4		Salaries	360,000.0	370,800.0	385,632.0	404,913.6
5		Benefits	133,200.0	137,196.0	142,683.8	149,818.0
6		Cost of office space	264,000.0	264,000.0	264,000.0	264,000.0
7		Total	757,200.0	771,996.0	792,315.8	818,731.6

The completed Budget sheet

Deliver

Print the model.

- Create a header showing the following *(See Appendix F for details)*:
    Page numbers
    Name of the model
    Date and time

- Make sure the page numbers are consecutive. *For tips on printing multiple sheet page numbers, see Appendix F.*

YOUR RESULTS

Original assumptions

[ ] Cost of office space, Year 3

[ ] Total budget, Year 3

Time for some What-If games!

1. What if the cost of office space rises to 135 per square foot in Years 2 and 3?

[ ] Cost of office space, Year 3

[ ] Total budget, Year 3

Change back to the original assumptions: 120 per square foot in all years.

2. What if Benefits rise to 40% of Salaries in Year 3?

[ ] Total budget, Year 3

Training for Finance

PART 2. FINANCIAL PROJECTIONS

CHALLENGE — OIL FIELD ANALYSIS

THE PROBLEM

You're evaluating an oil deal for Oilco. The oil company projects that 25,000,000 barrels of oil can be extracted from a field which costs $125,000,000 to buy. The current price of oil is $11 per barrel.

Here are the figures for percentage extracted per year and extraction costs as a percentage of revenues over the 5-year extraction period:

	Year 1	Year 2	Year 3	Year 4	Year 5
% extracted	10%	20%	30%	25%	15%
Costs % of revenues	40%	30%	25%	25%	25%

Calculate the following

Key results
- Total cash flows, Years 1 – 5
- IRR

Supporting calculations
- Number of barrels produced per year
- Revenues
- Costs of extraction
- Net profit

What-if scenario 1
What happens if the price of oil rises $1 a year after Year 1?

What-if scenario 2
What happens if the price of oil falls to $10 / barrel in Years 3, 4, and 5?

What-if scenario 3
What happens if the number of extractable barrels is really 20,000,000? Assume this number is discovered before drilling starts. Use the original oil price assumptions.

Hints

1. Place your assumptions and key results on one sheet. Put the calculations on a second sheet.
2. Show figures as thousands where appropriate.
3. Use the **IRR** function to calculate IRR. Review Problem Set 6 if you need help with this function.

© 1998 Adkins & Matchett

4. Try setting up a **Totals and Constants** column as below. You can put the initial cost (cost of the land) in it. It's also useful to total costs, revenues, or percentages as a check on your calculation.

		Totals and Constants	Year 1	Year 2
1	Oilco oil fields			
2	*Assumptions*			
3	Oil sale price/barrel ($)			

Totals and Constants column

YOUR RESULTS

Original assumptions

[   ] IRR

[   ] Total cash flows, Years 1 - 5

What-if scenario 1

What if the price of oil rises $1 a year after Year 1?

[   ] IRR

[   ] Total cash flows, Years 1 - 5

What-if scenario 2

What happens if the price of oil falls to $10 / barrel in Years 3, 4, and 5?

[   ] IRR

[   ] Total cash flows, Years 1 - 5

What-if scenario 3

What happens if the number of extractable barrels is really 20,000,000? Assume this fact is discovered before drilling starts. Use the original oil price assumptions.

[   ] IRR

[   ] Total cash flows, Years 1 - 5

SET 10   MULTI-SHEET PROJECTION

Model construction features

- Project a set of financial statements using multiple sheets
- Use a plug number to balance the balance sheet
- Use secondary calculations to derive

Excel features

- Multiple sheet formula construction
- Printing sheet page numbers on multiple sheets

CHALLENGE   PROJECT COPIOUS CORP. 3 YEARS

THE PROBLEM

Project Copious Corp's financial statement for 3 years. Use multiple sheets.

Create a separate sheet for each of these sections:

Assumptions

Calculations
Derive retained earnings

Income statement

Balance sheet
Use a cash plug formula to balance the balance sheet.

Cash flow statement
Make sure the change in cash on the cash flow statement matches the change in cash calculated from cash on the balance sheet.

Historical information and assumptions are on the next page.

What-if scenario 1
What if Copious increases its sales and taxes are reduced?

	Year 1	Year 2	Year 3
Sales growth	9.0%	10.0%	13.0%
Taxes % of Net inc. bef. taxes	26.0%	25.0%	24.0%

What-if scenario 2
Return to the original assumptions. What if Copious increases its assets?

	Year 1	Year 2	Year 3
Current assets	20.0%	20.0%	20.0%

What-if scenario 3
Return to the original assumptions. What if Copious increases liabilities?

	Year 1	Year 2	Year 3
Current liabilities	20.0%	20.0%	20.0%

© 1998 Adkins & Matchett

The grand finale

In this final problem set, you'll apply everything you've learned in this section. If you have problems, refer to the earlier problem sets and the Appendices.

Be sure to check your completed model against the checklist. You're not finished with the model until you're sure it's correct!

If you get stuck, check the answer in the back.

This is it! Knock yourself out!

Copious Corp. figures in thousands	Hist Year 0	Assumptions Proj Year 1	Proj Year 2	Proj Year 3
Income statement				
Sales growth		8%	8%	10%
COGS % of sales		68%	68%	68%
Operating expenses % of sales		24%	24%	24%
Taxes % of Net inc. before taxes		40%	40%	40%
Balance sheet				
Asset assumptions				
Current assets % of sales		18%	18%	18%
Fixed assets yearly growth		20%	20%	20%
Liabilities assumptions				
Current liabs. % of sales		15%	15%	15%
Long-term debt		250.0	300.0	350.0
Equity assumptions				
Capital stock		110.0	110.0	110.0

Assumptions for Copious Corp's projection

PART 2. FINANCIAL PROJECTIONS

Hmmmmm! How to proceed?

Copious Corp. Historical information

figures in thousands	Hist Year 0
Income statement	
Revenues	1,400.0
COGS	950.0
Gross profit	450.0
Operating expenses	340.0
Net income before taxes	110.0
Taxes	44.0
Net income	66.0
Balance sheet	
Assets	
Cash	378.0
Current assets	252.0
Net fixed assets	400.0
Total assets	630.0
Liabilities	
Current liabilities	210.0
Long-term debt	110.0
Equity	
Capital stock	110.0
Retained earnings	200.0
Total equity	310.0
Total L&E	630.0

As discussed in Problem Set 8, you will not show historical info for the Cash Flow Statement.

Here is a set of cash flow statement labels.

Cash flow statement
Net income
(Inc.) / Dec. in current assets
Inc. / (Dec.) in current liabilities
    Cash flow from operations

(Inc.) / Dec. in fixed assets
    Cash flow from investing activities

Inc. / (Dec.) in total debt
Inc. / (Dec.) in ???   *Which B/S account is missing? You fill it in.*
    Cash flow from financing activities

Net change in cash

Assumptions for Copious Corp's projection

© 1998 Adkins & Matchett

BUILD BUSINESS SPREADSHEETS USING EXCEL

I don't trust it until I've checked it!

Checklist

- ❏ No circular references
- ❏ No Excel error messages like **#REF!** or **#VALUE!**
- ❏ Cash flow statement foots with balance sheet
- ❏ Balance sheet balances
- ❏ Accounts look reasonable. Scan from left to right across each account. Do any accounts rise or fall sharply in the first projected year? There may be an error somewhere.
- ❏ No hard numbers in input formulas!
- ❏ Columns are consistent across all sheets (Year 1 data is in the same column on all sheets, for example)

Deliver

Print the entire model with a header showing your name, the name of the model, the date and time. Add a footer with page numbers.

HOW TO: PRINT MULTIPLE SHEETS

Page numbering multiple sheets
Select the sheets you want to print. Set up the header or footer for these sheets (you can do it for all the sheets by grouping the sheets first). The pages will automatically number themselves.

Or you can select **Entire Workbook** on the **Print** menu. That choice will also give you consecutive page numbers.

If you don't want to print an entire sheet
Notice the choice **Selection** on the **Print** menu. You can highlight part of a sheet and print it. But if you highlight and print sheets one by one, each sheet will say Page 1.

You can get around this problem by doing the following:

1. Go to **File Setup Sheet** and click in the **Print Area** box. Then click in the worksheet and drag over the selection you want to print.

2. If you do this on several sheets and then select those sheets, you can print the selections on each sheet and get consecutive page numbers, too.

Training for Finance

PART 2. FINANCIAL PROJECTIONS

YOUR RESULTS

Original assumptions

[ ] Net income in Year 3

[ ] Cash, Year 3

[ ] Retained earnings, Year 3

What-if Scenario 1
What if Copious increases its sales and taxes are reduced?

	Year 1	Year 2	Year 3
Sales growth	9.0%	10.0%	13.0%
Taxes % of Net inc bef. taxes	39.0%	38.0%	37.0%

[ ] Net income in Year 3

[ ] Cash, Year 3

[ ] Retained earnings, Year 3

What-if Scenario 2
Return to the original assumptions. What if Copious increases its assets?

	Year 1	Year 2	Year 3
Current assets	20.0%	20.0%	20.0%

[ ] Net income in Year 3

[ ] Cash, Year 3

[ ] Retained earnings, Year 3

In this scenario, *Cash* ❏ rose   ❏ fell   ❏ stayed the same.

What-if Scenario 3
Return to the original assumptions. What if Copious increases liabilities?

	Year 1	Year 2	Year 3
Current liabilities	20.0%	20.0%	20.0%

[ ] Net income in Year 3

[ ] Cash, Year 3

[ ] Retained earnings, Year 3

In this scenario, *Cash* ❏ rose   ❏ fell   ❏ stayed the same.

© 1998 Adkins & Matchett

Appendices

Appendix A: Efficiency

The best keyboard and mouse shortcuts

BEING EFFICIENT

If your job demands that you use Excel for several hours a day, you can't afford *not* to be efficient! The shortcuts in this Appendix are for you. If you use Excel only occasionally, you can afford to do things the long way.

The professional's key to efficiency

Use the keyboard, not the mouse. Excel pushes the mouse on new learners because it's easy. But if you want to really master Excel, take the time to learn the major keyboard shortcuts, for three reasons:

- **It's faster.** You don't have to pick your hand up off the keyboard, move it to the mouse, click, move back, etc.

- **You'll learn more.** Some of the more sophisticated options aren't easily available by mouse. If you want full power, lay off the icons and learn to use the menus the fast way: with keyboard shortcuts.

- **It's healthier.** If you're working for hours on end, the mouse is more likely to hurt your hand and wrist.

Should you use the mouse at all? Yes, of course! There are times when it's the best, fastest option available. You should definitely use the mouse to build formulas. NEVER type formulas!

OK, here they are...the best shortcuts, straight from the pros!

KEYBOARD SHORTCUTS

Functions and formulas

SUM function . . . . .ALT =

Edit

Edit a cell F2
Move the cursor quickly when editing a cell . . . . .CTRL ARROW, CTRL HOME, CTRL END
Apply or remove $ to make a cell reference
in a formula absolute or relative F4
                                        (Keep tapping it – there are 4 different positions)

| EFFICIENCY | APPENDIX A |

Move the cursor quickly

Move from one edge of a block of cells to the other . . .**CTRL+ARROW**
Note: the cursor moves until it detects the "edge" of a block of touching cells. If you jump off the end of a block of touching cells with CTRL+right arrow or CTRL+down arrow and there are no more occupied cells in the pointer's path, the pointer will fly until it hits the wall (the right side or bottom of the spreadsheet). To get back, try CTRL+left arrow or CTRL+up arrow.

Move to the top of the spreadsheet . . . .**CTRL+HOME**

Move from sheet to sheet . . . .**CTRL+PAGE UP** or **CTRL+PAGE DOWN**

Select cells

Select touching cells . . . .**SHIFT+ARROW**
Avoids the horrendous "runaway mouse" syndrome when you try to select cells that lie past the edge of the screen

Select entire row . . . .**SHIFT+SPACE BAR**

Select entire column . . . .**CTRL+SPACE BAR**

Common menu commands

Undo your last command . . . .**CTRL Z**
Copy . . . .**CTRL C**
Cut or move . . . .**CTRL X**
Paste . . . .**CTRL V**
Save . . . .**CTRL S**
Print . . . .**CTRL P**
Open a file . . . .**CTRL O**
Create a new file . . . .**CTRL N**
*You'll probably issue this command without intending to. It'll happen if you hit **CTRL** instead of **SHIFT** when you're trying to type **N**. If you do this, just close the empty file and keep going!*

Open the Format Cells menu . . . .**CTRL 1**

Other menu commands

Get to any menu . . . .**ALT**, then underlined letter of menu choice
If you try these commands a few times, your hands will start to remember them automatically.
Rename a sheet? **ALT o h r**

© 1998 Adkins & Matchett

EFFICIENCY   APPENDIX A

Useful function keys

Alter the absolute or relative nature of ....**F4** *Works this way when you're in* **EDIT** *mode*
a cell reference in a formula

Repeat the last formatting command ....**F4** *Works this way when you're NOT in* **EDIT** *mode*

Go to a cell or a range name **F5**

Force the spreadsheet to recalculate **F9**

Miscellaneous

Switch from one **spreadsheet** to ....**CTRL Tab**
another inside Excel

Switch from one **program** to ....**ALT Tab**
another (from Excel to Word, for
example)

MOUSE SHORTCUTS

Select cells

Select non-touching cells ....Click on a cell, hold down **CTRL**, click on a distant cell.
Only possible with the mouse.

Select non-touching cells in   Start the SUM function.
a SUM function   Click on the first cell you want to add.
                                          Hold down CTRL.
                                          Click on the next cell.
                                          And so forth.

166 Training for Finance

BUSINESS FORMULAS AND FUNCTIONS — APPENDIX B

APPENDIX B

Common business formulas and functions

Formulas

Apply a discount . . . . If a pair of $10 socks is offered at a 20% discount, how much is the discounted price? **Price * discount percentage**

Find a discount . . . . If a $300 cellular phone is selling for $240, how much is the discount? Find the difference between the discounted price and the full price. Then divide the difference by the full price. **$60 / $300**

Growth formula . . . . If last year's sales of 200 grow by 5%, what will this year's sales be? **Previous unit * (1 + growth factor)**

Take a percentage . . . . Sales are 400, and COGS is 65% of sales. **Key number (sales) * percentage**

Present value and future value formulas . . $PV = \dfrac{FV}{(1+r)^t}$ In Excel: **FV/(1+r)^t**

$FV = PV(1+r)^t$ In Excel: **PV*(1+r)^t**

Functions

What are functions? . . . . Functions are built-in formulas. You can use them anytime and anywhere in Excel.

Structure . . . . All functions have the same general structure:

=	**SUM**	**(arguments)**
formula symbol	name of function	specifications that show the function which cells to use

More about arguments . . . . The arguments tell the function which cells to act on.

Example: **=SUM(A1:A4,B5)**
Example: **=PV(rate,nper,pmt)** Commas separate arguments.
Example: **=IF(assets=liab_equities,C14,D22)** You can use cell references and range names in arguments.

Finding functions . . . . You can get to any function by either typing its name or picking it off a list of functions.

Icon: Find the **Paste Function** *(Excel 97)* **or Function Wizard** on the standard toolbar.
Menu: **Insert Function**

Paste Function *or* Function Wizard . . . . . . The function icon lists functions by category. Pick a category, then find the function you want under the Function Name list.

© 1998 Adkins & Matchett

BUSINESS FORMULAS AND FUNCTIONS   APPENDIX B

Functions within formulas . . . . .Put a function in a formula.   =C14-SUM(A12:A15)

Functions within functions . . . . .Put a function in another function.   =MAX(SUM(C24,D43),0)

Just make sure you get the number of parentheses right. You must have the same number of left and right parentheses.

Function troubleshooter . . . . .If you have a problem with a function, go through this checklist:
1. Do you have the right number of parentheses?
2. If you embedded a function inside another function, did you put in an extra = sign? Don't.
   Wrong =IF(=SUM(C4:C8,D14,0)
   Right =IF(SUM(C4:C8,D14,0)
3. Did you leave off an essential argument?

Shortcut . . . . .Type the name of the function yourself =AVERAGE(

Individual functions

SUM . . . .=SUM(cell1:cell4)   Adds a range of cells.
=SUM(cell1,cell2,cell7)   Adds individual cells.

When you issue the SUM function, it looks around for the nearest range of cells to add. First it looks up; if it finds no cells, it looks left.

	D	E	F
1			12
2			14
3			18
4	134	145	=SUM(F1:F3)

It also does not want to add another SUM function, so if a SUM function is in a column of numbers you want to add, the SUM function will stop selecting at that cell.

SUM shortcut .The best shortcut in Excel!   **ALT =**

SUM inside other formulas or functions . .You can use SUM functions inside other functions or formulas:
=SUM(B4:B8)–SUM(C18:C20)
One drawback: the shortcuts don't work. Neither the icon nor the **ALT =** shortcut will help you write the second SUM function in this example. You'll have to type the function name and parentheses yourself.

BUSINESS FORMULAS AND FUNCTIONS — APPENDIX B

SUM function tricks .... 1. You can override the SUM function's default selection and make it add any group of cells you want.

KEYBOARD	MOUSE
Arrow to the first cell.	Click on the first cell.
Hold down **SHIFT**.	Drag through the last cell.
Arrow to last cell in range.	

2. You can select cells that don't touch each other (aren't in a range).

KEYBOARD	MOUSE
Arrow to the first cell.	Click on the first cell.
Type a comma.	Hold down **CTRL**.
Arrow to the next cell.	Click on the next cell.

SUM across multiple sheets ....
1. You must add the same cell or range in all sheets.
2. Put your pointer in the cell where you want the sum to appear.
3. Issue the SUM command   =**SUM(**
4. Click on the first sheet's cell(s) to be summed.
5. Hold down **SHIFT**.
6. Click on the last sheet's tab.
7. **Enter**. Your across-sheet formula will look like this: =**SUM(Sheet1:Sheet4!A4)**

AVERAGE .... =**AVERAGE(cell1:cell4)**   Averages a range of cells
= **AVERAGE(cell1,cell2,cell7)** Averages individual cells

Averages cells that contain values

The AVERAGE function operates the same way the SUM function does. See the SUM function, above, for more info.

Warning!
=AVERAGE averages only cells that contain numbers!

IMPORTANT! What you should know about the AVERAGE function

	A
1	3
2	0
3	3
4	=AVERAGE(A1:A3) 2

AVERAGE with 0 in A2

	A
1	3
2	
3	3
4	=AVERAGE(A1:A3) 3

AVERAGE without 0 in A2

MAX .... Shows you the biggest number in a range of cells:
=**MAX(cell1:cell4)**

Shows you the biggest number in a list of individual cells:
=**MAX(cell1,cell2,cell7)**

MIN .... This function is the reverse of the MAX function.
=**MIN(cell1:cell4)**   Shows you the smallest number in a range of cells
=**MIN(cell1,cell2,cell7)**   Shows you the smallest number in a list of individual cells

You can often use **MAX** or **MIN** in place of a longer, more cumbersome **IF** statement.

© 1998 Adkins & Matchett

BUSINESS FORMULAS AND FUNCTIONS   APPENDIX B

IF	The IF function lets you automate a model by creating an IF, THEN, OTHERWISE statement. (IF this is true, THEN do this, OTHERWISE (if not true) do that.)
	Excel form of the IF statement: **=IF(statement, what to do if statement is true, what to do if statement is not true)**
Use words in IF statements	You can use words in the IF function. Enclose them in quotes: **=IF(Assets = L&E,"Balanced","Not balanced")** Note the position of the commas.

Operation signs

Equal to	=	Greater than or equal to	>=
Not equal to	<>	Less than	<
Greater than	>	Less than or equal to	<=

Financial functions

PV & FV *even cash flows* ....=**PV**(rate,nper,pmt,*fv,type*)
=**FV**(rate,nper,pmt,*pv,type*)

See Problem Set 5 for more information and examples

Important hints!
1. Always express **interest** and **term** in the same time units!
2. **PV** and **FV** are correct only for **even** cash flows! All payments must be the same amount.
3. Enter payments as negatives.

In case of trouble
☠ If your answer is a negative number, you probably didn't enter payments as negatives.
☠ If your answer is ridiculously small or large, you may not have adjusted your rate and interest entries so that they reflect the same time periods.

NPV *use for **uneven** cash flows*

NPV(rate,values)
Present value of stream of **uneven** cash flows. The payments can be uneven in size but not in time.
rate assumed interest rate
values spreadsheet range containing cash flows

See Problem Set 6 for more information and examples

Important note! Do not include the **initial payment** in the range of cash flows.

IRR Internal rate of return ....**IRR(values,guess)**
values Worksheet range containing cash flows. At least one of the cash flows must be negative.
guess Estimate of rate, expressed as a percentage. Optional. If you leave it out, Excel uses 10% as its guess.
Use the guess argument if the IRR is very large or very small.

See Problem Set 6 for more information and examples

Important note!
1. **Always** include the initial payment in the range of cash flows!
2. In case of a **#NUM!** Error message: Change your guess and recalculate.

Training for Finance

APPENDIX C
Excel troubleshooter and question guide

1. **How do I get rid of the wiggling box after I paste with CTRL V?**
   Press Escape. You can also press Enter, but that will paste a copy of the clipboard into your current cell.

2. **I suddenly found myself on a blank sheet. All my work disappeared.**
   Were you trying to type a capital N? You probably pressed the keyboard shortcut **CTRL N** by mistake. **CTRL N** brings up a fresh new sheet.
   To recover, just close the empty file. Your old file should be waiting for you.

   Or perhaps you moved to another sheet tab by mistake. Click on neighboring sheet tabs and see if you simply moved to another sheet by mistake.

3. **A number shows up as 0 in the spreadsheet, even though I can see it in the Edit bar.**
   Is the number less than .5? You've typed the number into a cell that's formatted as comma or currency with 0 decimal places, and it's rounded down.
   Just reformat the cell as percent or increase the number of decimal places.

4. **My cells are showing strange messages:**
   #########   The column's not wide enough for the format you are using.
   1E+08   That's scientific notation. Number too large for the cell (or too small).

5. **The word "Calculate" is showing up on the status bar.**
   Your **Tools Options Calculation** choices have been changed. Perhaps you've just opened a file whose settings were altered. At any rate, go to the **Tools Options Calculation** menu and check these settings:

   a. Is **Calculation** set to **Manual?** If Yes, change it back to **Automatic.**

   b. Is **Iteration** turned on? If Yes, you have an exotic, sophisticated condition in your spreadsheet. Right now, you shouldn't be building a spreadsheet that uses iteration. Turn off **Iteration**, find the circular reference, and get rid of it.

   If you've opened someone else's spreadsheet and found this condition, ask the creator to explain the use of iteration in this spreadsheet to you.

6. **I see the word Circular on the status bar.**
   You have a circular reference in an open spreadsheet. It may be in the spreadsheet you're looking at; it may be in another open model.

   See the Circular Reference section in Appendix H for a complete explanation.

7. **I can't get to menu commands sometimes.**
   Check to make sure you're not in the middle of editing a cell. If so, you can't get to most commands.

8. **I wrote a formula which shows me the result 0, and I know the answer is not zero.**
   a. Do you see the word Circular on the status bar? If you do, you have a circular reference. See No. 6, above. If you don't see Circular, go to point b.

   b. See No. 3, above.

9. **I copied a formula across and it shows 0's in the outlying cells.**
   You don't have a number in one of the cells the formula refers to. Trace the cell references and see what has happened.

10. **I can't see my...**
Toolbars	Go to **View Toolbars** and select at least one toolbar.
Status bar	Go to **Tools Options View** and select **Status Bar**.
Edit bar	Go to **Tools Options View** and select **Formula Bar**.

11. **My number pad doesn't type numbers.**
    Press the Num Lock key at the top of the number pad.

12. **I can't get my numbers to line up. Some of them have a space at the end. What's going on?**
    Read the appendix section on formatting, which explains everything.

13. **How do I get rid of the extra page break lines on the screen after I print?**
    You can try two options:
    a. Put your pointer in the row below or to the right of the page break line and see if you can give the **Insert Remove Page Break** command. If you can, the line will disappear.
    b. If a. doesn't work, check the **Insert Name Define** command and see if you find a range name called **Print_Area.** Delete it.

    Unfortunately, often neither of these options works. Just ignore the lines; they won't print out.

14. **The formulas suddenly appeared in the cells instead of the answer.**
    Four possibilities:
    1. You hit the space bar as you were starting to enter the formula, turning it into a label.
    2. You accidentally hit the ' apostrophe, which turns a formula into a non-computing label.
    3. You accidentally typed **CTRL ~**, which shows the formulas. Press it again to get back to the results.
    4. You checked **Formulas** on the **Tools Options View** menu. Uh-oh! Go turn it off. What you probably meant to check is **Formula Bar**. You *do* want to see that feature.

15. **My toolbars look strange** *or* **I can't find one of the standard icons.**
    Someone has customized your toolbars. Look in Appendix D for instructions on how to get the default icons back on your toolbars as well as how to customize them.

16. **Is there any way to...**
    a. **...erase formats like borders or special text formatting from a cell without erasing the contents?**
       Yes. Try **Edit Clear Formats**   ALT e a f
    b. **...copy a row to a column or vice versa?**
       Yes. **Copy**, then use **Edit Paste Special Transpose**
    c. **...copy the column widths from one sheet to another?**
       Sorry, no. But see d, below.
    d. **...copy a whole sheet?**
       Yes, try **Edit Move or Copy Sheet Create a Copy**
    e. **...change the width of part of a column instead of the whole column?**
       Sorry, no.
    f. **...keep the cursor from moving down after I press Enter?**
       Yes. Go to **Tools Options Edit** and and uncheck **Move Selection After Enter**.
    g. **...stop Excel from trying to type in labels for me?**
       Yes. Go to **Tools Options Edit** and and uncheck **Enable Autocomplete for Cell Values**.

APPENDIX D
Guide to formatting

GENERAL GUIDELINES

1. Keep it clean and simple. Businesspeople appreciate clarity and readability. Less clutter is always better.
2. Clients would usually rather see a complete financial statement on one sheet than extra white space.
3. Remember that readability and clarity are your two main formatting goals.
4. Your office may have a different format for numbers. If they don't, follow the suggestions below.
5. Don't put empty columns between columns of data unless it's required by your company. This practice will make it twice as hard to copy or edit formulas. A real timewaster.
6. Resist the temptation to use boxes and drop shadows. Unnecessarily fussy! Use bold and lines instead.

Number formats

1. **Never** center columns of numbers.
2. Business formatting puts negative numbers in parentheses. These formats show negatives in parentheses:
   Comma
   Currency
   Custom formats designed to show negative numbers in parentheses.
3. Don't use italics with numbers. They're harder to read.
4. Be very, very careful in choosing background or font colors. Stick to dark font colors and extremely pale patterns (color backgrounds). When you print colors on a black-and-white printer and then copy them, the numbers are hard to read. *(Translation: Impossible!)*

	A	B	C
1	Income statement		
2	Revenues	500	525
3	COGS	325	332
4	Depreciation	45	52
5	*Gross margin*	*130*	*141*

NO! 3 different fonts, colored bands, centered numbers, too many lines, italics for numbers

	A	B	C
1	**Income statement**		
2	Revenues	500	525
3	COGS	325	332
4	Depreciation	45	52
5	Gross margin	130	141

YES! Clean, clear, simple, readable

Text formats

1. Use bold and font size changes to make headings stand out.
2. Use italics sparingly with headings, but not with numbers (see *Number formats*, above).
3. Right- or center-align headings over columns of numbers.
4. Use one, perhaps two fonts at most, in a file. Avoid "cute" or fancy fonts.

FORMATTING   APPENDIX D

Suggestions

1. You can't use the TAB key to indent as you would in a word processing program. Try using a narrow column for indenting (example below), or use the Indent feature (Excel 97only, **Format Cells Alignment**).
2. Make sections stand out by using bold and larger font sizes.
3. Use lines sparingly. A good place to put them is above major subtotals.
4. Indent subtotals by using the space bar. Crude but effective.

	A	B	C
1		**Revenues**	
2		Revenues	1,550
3		COGS	990
4		Depreciation	75
5		Gross margin	485
6		**Expenses**	
7		SG&A	340
8		Amortization	15
9		Other	38
10		EBIT	92

Simple but effective

Formatting with icons

For most formatting commands, you have a choice of icons or menus. You can either click on icons with the mouse or go through the menus with either the mouse or the keyboard. The next section, HOW TO, will show you both options.

If you've just purchased and installed Excel, you will be able to find icons on their appropriate toolbars. But if you are using a program that has already been used, you may not find the icons where you expect to. The other person has customized the toolbars.

Restore default toolbar settings . . . . . Go to **View Toolbars.** Select the toolbars you want to use, then **Reset**. Any customized settings that have been made will disappear and the default icons will be reestablished.

Customize the toolbars . . . . .Even if you're not an icon addict, you should customize your toolbars. You'll find some icons indispensable, and you'll want them on your toolbar at all times. You can also remove a lot of junk that you don't use. If you use keyboard shortcuts, you won't need most of the standard icons.
Try to customize your icons so that you have only one toolbar showing. You can use the space to see more of your model.

Use the mouse   Click the right mouse button on any icon. You'll get a special menu. Select **Customize**. Select a category and find the icon(s) you want. Use the mouse to drag them onto the toolbar. Drop them anywhere you like. They'll elbow the other icons aside to make room for themselves.

FORMATTING — APPENDIX D

HOW-TO

Text formatting

FONT CONTROLS	MENUS / KEYBOARD	ICONS / MOUSE
Font	**Format Cells Font** Gives you complete control over fonts and their characteristics **CTRL 1**	Icons on Formatting toolbar *Operate like on-off switch* Use the Underscore icon or the Borders icon, also on the Formatting toolbar
Size	**SHIFT CTRL P** then enter font size	
Bold	**CTRL B** *Operates like on-off switch*	
Italics	**CTRL I** *Operates like on-off switch*	
Underscore	**CTRL U** *Operates like on-off switch*	
Underscoring numbers	Try underscoring a number. Notice that the underscore doesn't stretch to the edges of the cell. If you want the underscore to reach the edge of the cell, use **Format Cells Borders**.	

ALIGNMENT

Alignment works on both labels and numbers.

Left, right, center	**Format Cells Alignment**	Icons on Formatting toolbar *Operate like on-off switch*
Alignment across columns	**Format Cells Alignment Center Across Selection** First select the cells you want to center a title across. Then execute the command.	First select the cells you want to center a title across. Then select Center Across Columns icon on the Formatting toolbar.

CELL BORDERS AND PATTERNS

You can color the insides of cells and put borders around part or all of them. Business spreadsheets sometimes use borders and *(very very pale)* color to mark assumption cells.

Borders	**Format Cell Borders** Gives you complete control over thickness, color and line position	Borders icon on Formatting toolbar Select the border you need *A good shortcut*
Patterns	**Format Cell Patterns**	Color icon on Formatting toolbar *A good shortcut*

175 Training for Finance

Number formatting

Business formats . . . . Business formats commonly show numbers as follows:

- 0, 1, or 2 decimal places for non-percentage figures
- Negative numbers in (parentheses)
- 0's visible as 0's rather than - dashes
- Negative and positive numbers aligned on the decimal point

1,234.0
(1,234.0)
0.0

How to manipulate formats

Copy formats   You can copy a format to other cells several ways:

Keyboard	Mouse
Copy a cell containing the format you like. **CTRL C**	Click on the cell whose format you want to copy.
Select the cell or cells you want to format.	Click on the Format Painter icon. It looks like a paintbrush.
Go to **Edit Paste Special** and select **Format**. **ALT e s t**	Select the cell or cells you want to format.

When you copy a cell you copy the format too   You can always copy the cell that contains a format you like, then type over the original entry.

Delete formats   If you delete the contents of a cell, is the format deleted too? NO.

Use the **Edit Clear Formats** command to delete formats without deleting the other contents of a cell.   **ALT e a f**

Keyboard commands . . . . Enter the number. Go to **Format Cells** (*CTRL 1*) and select from dozens of formats, or customize your own.

  PRO   You can get exactly what you want.
  CON   Slower than the mouse

Automatic formatting . . . . Type the format as you enter the number:
Type $1,234.00 in an unformatted cell

Note: Automatic formatting only works in an unformatted cell which has the **General** format.

  PRO   Easy
  CON   Doesn't give you complete control.
           Can't revise all the formatting at once. Have to do it on a cell-by-cell basis.

FORMATTING   APPENDIX D

What's the difference?

Automatic comma vs. Icon comma

Look at the difference between the Automatic comma format and the icon format:

	A
1	Automatic
2	1,234
3	23
4	Comma
5	1,234
6	23

Notice how the automatic numbers line up against the right edge of the cell? The Comma format numbers have a little space between the last number and the right edge of the cell.

Negative numbers

Why the space in the comma format?
Look at the negative number in each format.

	A	B
1	Automatic	-1,234.1
2	Comma	(1,234.1)

The Comma format puts negative numbers in parentheses. The parentheses take up space. The extra space you see at the end of positive numbers helps the Comma format line up positive and negative numbers with decimal points.

Menu formats

The zero problem

Enter a zero in a cell and click the Comma format.

	A
1	-

Comma icon

The 0 is not visible in the cell. Many businesses like to see zeros.

Put the pointer on the 0 and go to **Format Cells Number**. Select the **Number** Category, then select a sample that shows negative numbers in parentheses.

	A
1	0

Number format

The $ problem

Enter a number in a cell and format it as Currency by clicking on the $ icon. Notice the position of the dollar sign.

	A
1	$ 123.00

Currency icon

Put the pointer on your number and go to **Format Cells Number**. Select the **Currency** Category, then select a sample that shows negative numbers in parentheses.

	A
1	$123.00

Currency format

Now look at the position of the dollar sign.

177 Training for Finance

FORMATTING   APPENDIX D

The Format Cell command . . . . . . If you want to learn how to control your formats precisely, learn to use this menu. It gives you complete control over your formats.

Using the Custom format

You can figure out the other categories on your own. The **Custom** category is another story.

Look at the list of formats under **Custom**. The best way to learn this bewildering array of codes is to apply different formats to several cells and see what happens.

Custom format codes

Here are some custom codes that might be useful to you:

Comma with 1 decimal place   #,##0.0_);(#,##0.0)
zero values will appear as 0.0

Comma with 1 decimal place,
negative numbers in red   #,##0.0_);[Red](#,##0.0)

Percentage, 1 decimal place,
negative numbers in parentheses   0.0%_);(0.0%)

Examples	0	-1234	0.4	-0.4
#,##0.0_);(#,##0.0)	0.0	(1,234.0)	0.4	(0.4)
$ icon	$ -	$ (1,234.00)	$ 0.40	$ (0.40)
Currency category	$0.00	($1,234.00)	$0.40	($0.40)
% icon	0%	-NA-	40%	-40%
0.0%_);(0.0%)	0.0%	-NA-	40.0%	(40.0%)

What does it MEAN?

Heaven for techno-geeks:

    #,##0.0_);(#,##0.0)

\#   Don't print a number if no number appears in this position.

0   Print 0 if no number appears in this position.

_   Leave a space at the end of the number exactly as wide as the next character. See *More about the _) code*, below.

)   The character whose width should be left at the end of the number. See *More about the _) code*, below.

;   Separates positive format from negative format.

Where to get more info

These codes listed above are probably the most useful for you. You can discover many more codes if you use Excel's help. They're tucked away out of sight but you can find them. Go to the Index and find *Formatting numbers*, then *custom number formats*, then *custom number formats* again to get more codes.

More about the _) code

Here's what the _) code does. It lines up numbers so that negative and positive numbers in parentheses align properly over the decimal point.

1,234.0	Comma style
(1,234.0)	Comma style
1,234.0	Automatic style

The first two numbers are formatted with the Comma style, which includes the _) code. Notice how they align to the decimal point. The third number is in General style (no format applied yet). Notice how it does not align with the negative number.

© 1998 Adkins & Matchett   **178**

FORMATTING   APPENDIX D

The default icon formats		The icons are preset with Excel's default formats, called styles.
,	**Comma** icon	Accounting format. Negatives in parentheses, commas in thousands place. Zeros show as - lines. Control decimal places with the Increase or Decrease Decimals icons.
$	**Currency** icon	Accounting format. Currency sign aligned toward left, away from number. Negatives in parentheses, commas in thousands place. Zeros show as - lines. Control decimal places with the Increase or Decrease Decimals icons.
%	**Percent** icon	Simple percent. Negatives shown without parentheses.
	Increase decimals icon	Increases decimal places with each click.
	Decrease decimals icon	Decreases decimal places with each click.

More about styles — The default icons are also the default styles. You can see a list of these styles by going to **Format Style**.

Create your own style — You can create your own styles, which is very helpful if you use complex custom formats. Two ways:

The easy way — Create your custom format for a cell on your worksheet. *Important!* Leave your pointer right on that cell.

Go to **Format Style** and type a name for your format in the **Style Name** box. You'll immediately see Style Includes (By Example). Excel is looking at the cell's format and will use the cell as an example of the new style you want to create.

The precise way — Go directly to **Format Style**. Type a new name in the **Style Name** box. Then go to **Modify** and set up your formats.

The power of using this method is that you can turn off other **Style** specifications such as the font or border characteristics, and you can give your new style characteristics other than numeric, such as pattern or alignment.

Power Style tips

Install the Style icon . . . . For full style power, install a special Style icon on your toolbar. Your custom styles will be available on a little pull-down menu.

Copy custom styles — If you develop a good set of styles, you can copy them from file to file.
Open the file with the styles in it.
Open the file you want to copy the styles to. In this un-Styled file, go to Format Styles and select **Merge**.
Follow the directions to bring your custom styles over into the current file.
Your file with the custom styles in it must be open!

Change the formatting icons — If you modify the default styles, the style icons will reflect your modifications!

179   Training for Finance

APPENDIX E
Other useful commands and features

Edit Paste Special

You must copy something before you can access this great command, which lets you do all sorts of useful things.

When you copy a cell, you copy everything about it: formula, format, notes (if any). **Edit Paste Special** lets you paste part of the copy instead of everything. You can paste only the formats, only the formulas, the results of the formulas.

Here's a guide to the most-used features of **Edit Paste Special**.

FEATURE	PASTES...	USE
All	...everything.	
Formulas	...just the formula.	Lets you paste a formula into a pre-formatted cell, or lets you paste a formula without pasting its format.
Values	...hard numbers. The results of formulas, not the formulas themselves.	Useful for copying quick derivations as hard numbers for assumptions
Formats	...just the cell format.	Copy complex formats quickly. Same function as the Format Painter icon.
Comments / Notes	...comments or notes *(non-Excel 97)*	Useful if you have comments or notes that are almost exactly alike.
Operation choices	Lets you add /subtract/ multiply/ divide a copy into another cell.	Useful for merging sets of data if you don't need to see their sources.
Transpose	...a row to a column or a column to a row	Useful if you change your mind about a column of numbers and want to make it a row, or vice versa.

Special cautions

That wiggling box — Notice the wiggling box that remains even after you use Edit Paste Special? When you use Paste Special, the copy does not leave the clipboard. You can paste one part of the copy, then move to another cell and paste another part.

Careful! — Be careful not to hit Enter after you've used **Paste Special**. The full copy is still sitting on the clipboard!

Remove the box — To remove the wiggling box, press **Escape**.

| USEFUL COMMANDS | APPENDIX E |

Commands for deleting and clearing

Clear command on the Edit menu

Clear.................... **Clear** is a great command. It lets you erase everything in a cell: formulas, formats, contents, notes. You can also choose to erase only part of the contents of a cell.

KEYBOARD SHORTCUT	COMMAND	ACTION
ALT e a a	All	Deletes everything, including formats
ALT e a f	Formats	Removes just the formatting. This command is worth learning!

Caution You'll find a **Clear Contents** command on the Mouse menu (click the right mouse button in the spreadsheet). It works like the **Delete** key and is for diehard mouse operators. It is *not* the same as this **Clear** command.

Deleting with the Mouse menu

Clear contents............. Works like the **Delete** key. Does not remove formatting.

Delete... .... Takes you into the **Delete Cells** / **Rows** / **Columns** dialog box.
  Warning Do not use this command casually! Know what you're doing before you use it.

Deleting cells, rows, and columns

Danger! Danger!............. These commands can disrupt your whole spreadsheet! Why? Because you are deleting entire cells, rows and columns, not just their contents.

Effect on formulas........... If you delete a cell that a formula uses, the formula will be destroyed. You'll see the message **#REF!** in the formula cell. You will have to stop and rebuild the formula before your spreadsheet can work again.

Example

	A	B	C	
1		Retained earnings		
2		Retained earnings, beginning amt.	1,400.0	
3		Net income	340.0	
4		Dividends	85.0	
5		Retained earnings, ending amt.	1,655.0	=C2 + C3 - C4

What will happen if you delete Cell C3?

181 Training for Finance

	A	B	C	
1		Retained earnings		
2		Retained earnings, beginning amt.	1,400.0	
3		Net income	85.0	
4		Dividends	#REF!	=C2 + #REF! - C3
5		Retained earnings, ending amt.		

Here's what happens:

1. The cells below the deleted cell move up. Notice that the Dividends amount now sits across from the Net income label.

2. Because the original reference to the amount of 340 has been deleted, the formula has "lost its mind" and can't do anything but show a **#REF!** message. You have to rebuild the formula to make it work properly.

Now that you know the dangers, here's how to do it!

Delete cells . . . . Select the cell(s) first. Then go to the Delete menu

Shift cells left or up?   When you delete a cell, something has to fill the gap. You can pull the cells to the right of the deleted cell over to the left (Shift cells left) or you can pull the cells below the deleted cell up (Shift cells up). You choose!

                                            KEYBOARD   **MOUSE**

Delete rows   You can select the row(s) first, or not.   You can select the row(s) first, or not.

                                            To select the entire row(s):   *To select the row(s):*
                                            SHIFT spacebar   Click on the row number(s).

                                            Delete the row(s)   *When you have selected the row:*
                                            ALT e d   Select **Delete** on the mouse menu

                                            Without the entire row(s) selected: *Without the row(s) selected:*
                                            ALT e d r   Select **Delete** on the mouse menu.
                                                                                                Select **Entire Row**

Delete columns   *To select column(s):*   *As above*
                                            CTRL spacebar
                                          As above

Serjes Fill

What is it? . . . . Series Fill lets you create a series of numbers easily.

How it works   Excel needs to know what series you have in mind, so give it a pattern to follow by inputting the first two numbers in your series. You can input either in a column or a row.

USEFUL COMMANDS   **APPENDIX E**

See the examples in Problem Set 2 for more information.	Excel also recognizes several word sequences, like days of the week and months of the year. Some typical series:

First two cells	Excel continues the series with:
1 2	3 4 5
6 4	2 0 -2
Mon Tue	Wed Thu Fri
Qtr 1 Qtr 2	Qtr 3 Qtr 4 Qtr 1
Jan Feb	Mar Apr May

Customize your own fills. . . . . . . Go to **Tools Options Custom Lists** and create your own series fills.

Range names

What are range names? . . . . Range names are names you can give to a cell or range of cells.
Be sure you also read the Pro's and Con's section, below, before you start using them.

What do range names do? . . . . . . Range names have two primary uses:
1. Navigation. You can range name a distant location and then use the **Goto (F5)** key to move there quickly. The range name is easier to remember or to find than a cell address.
2. Formula construction. You can use range names in formulas. Use one anywhere you'd use a cell reference.

Acceptable range names . . . . . . 1. You can't use spaces in a range name, so keep them short.
If you have to use two words, either run them together or connect them with an underscore:
   BalanceSheet   **Balance_Sheet**
2. Your range name should be readable. It's really not very helpful to read a range name like this:
   Bsprevyrdn12
3. You're restricted to 15 characters.

Create a range name. . . . . There are almost too many ways to create range names.

Use the Name Box
1. Put your pointer on the cell or range you want to name.
2. Click the current address in the Name box (box to the left of the Edit bar. You'll see the cell address in the name box.
3. Type a one-word name.

Use the menu, Option 1
1. Highlight the cell or range you want to name.
2. Go to **Insert Name Define** and type the name you want to use.

Option 2.
Type the range name you want to use in a cell next to the range you're defining. You can place the name above, below, to the right or left of the range you're naming.

PRO   This method lets you use labels as range names.

183 Training for Finance

USEFUL COMMANDS

APPENDIX E

CON Often, your labels will be too long or will contain unacceptable spaces. You're better off writing new labels to one side of your ranges.

Delete a range name............ The only way to delete a range name is through the **Insert Name Define** menu. Select the range name and use the **Delete** button.

Find range names............. If a spreadsheet contains range names, you can find them in several places:
1. The **Name Box**. Open up the Name box (to the left of the Edit bar) by clicking on the arrow beside it. You'll see a list of all the range names in the file.
2. The **Goto** dialog box. Press **F5** or **CTRL G**.
3. The **Insert Name** menus.

Handy shortcut [F3]   When you're constructing a formula, press **F3** to get a list of range names. You can paste any range name into the formula by selecting it.

What you MUST KNOW about range names .... Single-cell range names behave differently from named ranges when they are copied.

	A	B	C	D
1	Budget	Year 1	Year 2	Year 3
2	Increase in personnel	4%	5%	6%
3	Inflation	3%	4%	5%

Range names, 1

Range names, 1 shows two named ranges:

Multi-cell range: B2:D2   PERSONNEL
Single-cell range: B3   INFLATION   Notice that this range doesn't include all years.

Look what happens when you create formulas:

	A	B	C	D
1	Budget	Year 1	Year 2	Year 3
2	Increase in personnel	4%	5%	6%
3	Inflation	3%	4%	5%
4				
5	=PERSONNEL	4%		
6	=INFLATION	3%		

Range names, 2

So far, so good. You can type =PERSONNEL in B5 and it will show you what's in B2.

What happens when you copy the range names?

	A	B	C	D
1	Budget	Year 1	Year 2	Year 3
2	Increase in personnel	4%	5%	6%
3	Inflation	3%	4%	5%
4				
5	=PERSONNEL	4%	5%	6%
6	=INFLATION	3%	3%	3%

Range names, 3

Very important to know! A single-cell range name copies like an absolute reference. A multi-cell range name copies like a mixed cell address, in this case B$2. See **Absolute reference** for more information about copying formulas.

© 1998 Adkins & Matchett

USEFUL COMMANDS

APPENDIX E

Pros and cons		At first, range names seem like one of the greatest spreadsheet features ever. Many introductory Excel classes will urge you to use them freely. But not so fast! There are some serious drawbacks to range names.
PRO	✓	Great for single cells that hold unchanging constants. An easy way to solve the absolute reference problem.
	✓	Fine for short, simple spreadsheets.
	✓	When used sparingly, are good at documenting formulas. You can actually read the formula in English instead of in cell references.
CON	✗	Range names make formula construction easier, but that may not be helpful to someone who has to master the intricacies of complex formula construction. My opinion: you'll gain a more intuitive understanding of modeling if you use cell references, at least while you're learning.
	✗	The more range names you use, the less benefit you get from them. 1. Your chances of using the wrong range name in a formula rise as the number of range names rises. When you're building formulas in a big model by picking from a list of 80 range names, you will almost certainly pick the wrong name from time to time. If you click on cell references, at least you know what you're getting. 2. Your formulas become so long and wordy that they're hard to read or edit. 3. You'll end up using abbreviations that are more confusing than a cell reference. Is the formula below really clear and easy to read? **=97yr_dn*prev_npe_+curr_slsrt**
	✗	You can't build mixed-reference formulas with range names.
	✗	*When ranges, not single cells, are named:* You can't use range names in growth formulas that refer to a figure in a different column.
	✗	If you ever lose or delete your range names, all formulas that were built with them are ruined.
	✗	Range names of any sort slow down your proofreading. Although it's just as easy to make a mistake and put the wrong range name into a formula as it is to click on the wrong cell, it's three times as hard to find the error when you're proofreading your work.

Absolute and relative reference

You MUST KNOW	If you are to move past the level of amateur, you must understand absolute and relative reference, the key to masterful formula construction. Absolute and relative references control how formulas act when they're copied.
Normal copy function	Normally, if you copy a formula in Excel, it copies with *relative references*. In other words, the formula copies as a pattern of cell references, not as a set of cell addresses. Look at the examples on the next page.

USEFUL COMMANDS

APPENDIX E

	A	B	C	D	E
1	Budget	All years	Year 1	Year 2	Year 3
2	Inflation	3%			
3	Salaries		500	550	610
4	Benefits		200	220	245
5	Personnel expenses		700	=SUM(C3:C4)	
6	Adjusted for inflation		721	=C5 * (1 + B2)	

Formulas for Year 1

Year 1 is fine. Both formulas work the way they should.

What happens when you copy the Personnel expenses SUM function in C5?

	A	B	C	D	E
1	Budget	All years	Year 1	Year 2	Year 3
2	Inflation	3%			
3	Salaries		500	550	610
4	Benefits		200	220	245
5	Personnel expenses		700	770	855

=SUM(C3:C4)   =SUM(D3:D4)   =SUM(E3:E4)

The formulas for the *Personnel expenses* copies

Relative references at work ...... The formula copies accurately. It does **not** copy C3:C4 across. It copies a **pattern of cell relationships**: "Add the two cells directly above the formula cell." When the pattern copies across, it is accurate for Years 2 and 3.

What happens when the inflation adjustment formula is copied across?

	A	B	C	D	E
1	Budget	All years	Year 1	Year 2	Year 3
2	Inflation	3%			
3	Salaries		500	550	610
4	Benefits		200	220	245
5	Personnel expenses		700	770	855
6	Adjusted for inflation		721	770	855

=C5*(1+B2)   =D5*(1+C2)   =E5*(1+D2)

The formulas for the *Inflation adjustment* copies

When relative reference .... The formula copied normally. It copied the pattern: "Cell above * (1 + the
doesn't work   cell one column to the left and 4 rows up)." But in this case, the copies produce the wrong answer. The copies in Columns D and E refer to empty cells

The reference to *Personnel expenses* copied accurately. You want that one to "float," or shift from column to column as it is copied across.
It's the reference to *Inflation %* that didn't copy accurately.

© 1998 Adkins & Matchett

| USEFUL COMMANDS | APPENDIX E |

The solution . . . . You must fix the reference to B2 (make it absolute) so that it doesn't change when the formula is copied. Here's how the absolute reference looks and copies correctly:

	A	B	C	D	E
1	Budget	All years	Year 1	Year 2	Year 3
2	Inflation	3%			
3	Salaries		500	550	610
4	Benefits		200	220	245
5	Personnel expenses		700	770	855
6	Adjusted for inflation		721	770	855

=C5*(1+$B$2)   =D5*(1+$B$2)   =E5*(1+$B$2)

These absolute copies work!

$ signs = absolute . . . . The code for absolute reference is $. You can reference a cell 4 ways:

   B2   Both row and column copy relatively
   $B$2   Row and column references remain fixed.

These are the most commonly used variations on absolute reference. You can also used mixed cell addressing:

   $B2   Column remains fixed; row "floats."
   B$2   Column "floats," row remains fixed.

Most of the time you won't use these subtle variations, but in some complex models you may find that only a mixed cell reference will do.

Technically, you could use **B$2** in the example above.

The $ shortcut **F4**   Works only when you're creating or editing a formula. Press **F4** and watch what happens.

Be sure you press **F4** four times to see all the variations you get. You can apply all 4 reference combinations by continuing to press **F4**.

Other commands

View Zoom Custom . . . . Lets you adjust the size of the screen within the window.

Format Row / Column Hide. . . . . . Lets you hide a row or column. Highlight across the unhidden columns and use **Format Row / Column Unhide** to reveal the hidden columns or rows again. Watch out -- this could get confusing to your audience.

Data Group and Outline Group . . A better alternative to hiding rows and columns. Try it and see! To remove it, use **Data Group Ungroup**.

187 Training for Finance

APPENDIX F
Printing in Excel

HOW A BUSINESS PRINTOUT SHOULD LOOK

Clear and informative

Headers and footers — Your business printouts should always include either a header or footer containing this information:
- Date and time
- Page number and number of total pages (Page 1 of 3)
- The name of the spreadsheet

Depending on your audience, you might also want to include:
- Your name
- The sheet name (if you are using multiple sheets)
- The file location

Column / row headings, gridlines — You can print your work out either with or without gridlines and row and column headings.

When they're useful — Use gridlines and row and column headings on your proofreading copy so you can check it carefully.

When to avoid them — Don't show row and column headings in your final beauty copy for your client (your boss, your customer). You may or may not want to show gridlines. Make your own decision. Most companies now print final copies without them.

Formatting — See comments in Appendix D on formatting for additional guidelines.

General comments

Print Preview — Use **Print Preview** to check your print setup before you print. You'll save time as well as paper.

Experiment — The best way to find out how the printing commands work is to play with the settings and then **Print Preview** the results.

PRINTING APPENDIX F

FILE PAGE SETUP

Customize your printouts . . . . Use the **File Page Setup** command to customize your printouts. All the commands below are on one of the four **Page Setup** menus. I'm only going to cover the really useful or interesting commands. You can figure out everything else on your own.

The Page menu

Portrait or Landscape? . . . . Portrait prints the paper out longways.
Landscape prints the paper out sideways.

Scaling . . . . Use this if you want to squeeze your data onto one or more pages. You can reduce the size with the **Adjust to** command, or you can use **Fit to** to tell Excel to fit it on one page.

     Tip The **Fit to** command is great if you have a printout with one extra column on a second page. Tell Excel to Fit to 1 page wide by zero pages tall. Erase the number in the **by ____ tall** box.

The Margins menu Self-explanatory

The Header/Footer menu

About headers and footers . . . . You can create one-line or multiple-line headers and footers. Try to keep your headers and footers to one line to save room.
The custom header and footer creation boxes have three parts that let you center and left- and right-align text.

Left-aligned	Centered	Right-aligned

Header/footer icons . . . . Use the icons to insert special codes in your header or footer.

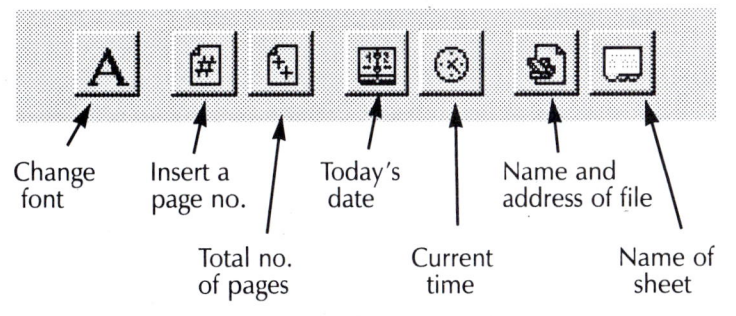

    Change Insert a Today's Name and
    font page no. date address of file

       Total no. Current Name of
       of pages time sheet

You could also type the codes if you wanted to.

© 1998 Adkins & Matchett **189**

PRINTING   APPENDIX F

A typical footer	Here's a typical footer:
The codes	&(File)　　　　　　　　Page &(Page) of &(Pages)　　　　　&(Date) &(Time)
The results	PRINT.XLS　　　　　　　　Page 1 of 3　　　　　　March 30, 1998 12:44)

The sheet menu

What it offers you . . . . This menu has a lot of valuable features. It controls the printing of:
　　　　　　　　　　　　　　　　Gridlines
　　　　　　　　　　　　　　　　Row and column headings
　　　　　　　　　　　　　　　　Other interesting features

Print titles . . . . This feature lets you specify rows to print at the top of every printed page.

　　A great feature　　　　　Don't ever copy your title rows down the page! Use this feature instead. Click the mouse in the **Rows to Repeat at Top** box. Then use the mouse to select the rows you want to see at the top of every page.

Print Area . . . . If you always want to print part of the spreadsheet, not all of it, you should use the **Print Area** feature. If you specify the print area in this box, Excel will always print that area.
　　　　　　　　　　　　　　　You can use a range name to specify the area you want printed, or you can use the mouse.
　　　　　　　　　　　　　　　1.　Click in the **Print Area** box.
　　　　　　　　　　　　　　　2.　Use the mouse to select the area you want to print.

Page breaks . . . . You can insert page breaks to control what's printed on a multi-page spreadsheet.
　　　　　　　　　　　　　　　Use the command **Insert Page Break** to place a page break wherever you want. The page break appears in the row above the pointer position. You should see a line of dashes showing its position.

Vertical page breaks . . . . You can place a vertical page break by selecting an entire column. The page break appears to the left of the selected column.

Remove page breaks. . . . . Remove page breaks by placing your pointer in any cell below the page break. If you're removing a vertical page break, place your pointer to the right of the page break line.
　　　　　　　　　　　　　　　Go to the **Insert** menu and you'll see that the **Page Break** menu choice now reads **Remove Page Break**. Select the command.

Those pesky page break lines . . . After you preview a print or actually print something, you'll see page break lines on the screen. They show how much of your spreadsheet fits on one page. They won't show on your printout. They will usually disappear when you close and reopen your file.

Print_Area page break lines　　　If you define a print area using the **File Page Setup Sheet Print Area** command, you actually create a temporary range name called **Print_Area**.
　　　　　　　　　　　　　　　If you look at your list of range names and find **Print_Area**, you can delete it and the page break lines will also disappear. Deleting the **Print_Area** range name does not affect your **Page Setup** specs.

APPENDIX G
The A-B-C-D of spreadsheet design

Overview

The larger and more complex your model is, the more important it is for you to plan your model *before* you sit down at the keyboard. You can build a simple model intuitively, or a model that's like dozens of others you've already built, but for something new or complex, sit down and apply some analytical skills before you start.

A   Analyze

Before you begin

1. What **result** should your model produce?
2. Do you have all the **information** you need?
3. What are the **assumptions**?
4. Are any of the assumptions **constants**? In other words, variables that will *never change*? These assumptions could be hard-coded in formulas.
   Examples: 7 days in a week
   24 hours in a day
5. Will any assumptions will remain the same throughout the life of the model? For instance, in an oil deal you might have an assumption for the initial cost of the land. You would want to be able to change the assumption, but it needs to appear only once.
   Examples: A company's fiscal year end
   The interest rate on a loan
6. Will you need intermediate calculations?
7. Does your client need to see the intermediate calculations?

B   Build

Layout decisions .... Before you start building, think of how you will lay out the model.

Sectional design	Single sheet?	Short single-section models
	Multiple sheet?	Lengthy, complex models with several sections
Layout structure	Horizontal layout?	Projections with many years
	Vertical layout?	Budgets with few years and many categories
Intermediate calculations	Visible?	Information important in itself
	Hidden away?	Information important only in reaching the end result
Flexibility	Maximum?	Assumptions for each time period
	Minimum?	One assumption for all time periods

A B C D APPENDIX G

Special multiple sheet tip		If you are building a complex multiple-sheet model, make sure all relevant sheets contain the same set of columns in the same order and position! In other words, Year 1 is Column D on all sheets, not Column D on the Income Statement and Column E on the Balance Sheet.
Building sequence.	1.	Input labels and historical information. Set up special styles early. Perform basic number formatting and column width adjustment as you work. But leave anything fancy for last.
	2.	Build assumptions (assumption block, input area, constants page – the area can have many different names).
	3.	Build the formulas.
TIPS		Use the mouse for formula building. Don't use hard-coded assumptions in output formulas! Avoid overusing range names in formulas. *(Avoid range names entirely!)* Split complex calculations into single steps.

C Check

Why you *must* check	The bigger and more complicated your model is, the more likely you'll commit a fatal error and not notice it. A pro never trusts a model just because it's producing an answer and it's good-looking. Always check your work.
Check now, check later	Don't wait till you're through! Check each section, or if you're modeling a projection, check each year before you copy it across.
Use the checklists	See Appendix H for complete checklists, guidelines, and common errors.

D Document, Decorate, Deliver

Document.		Make sure your client understands your model.
	1.	Clear, concise labels for all accounts.
	2.	Assumptions visible so everyone can see them.
	3.	Complex calculations split into single steps.
Decorate.	1.	Keep it clean and simple.
	2.	Apply underlining, patterns, colors, etc., **last**
	3.	Remember that you can waste hours producing fun but pointless charts, graphs, colored cells, text boxes, little diagrams, and goodness knows what more. Keep all that stuff to a minimum and concentrate your precious time on building a clean, clear, reliable model that you have proofed and checked.
Deliver		Make sure your model looks its best before it goes to your boss or client.
Cover sheet		Prepare a cover sheet on the first sheet of your model. Show your name, the name of the model, the date, your phone number, a guide to the model, information about the company you're modeling, and a list of special features a user should know about.
Beauty save		Before your final save, "home" the cursor in the upper corner of each sheet. Move to your cover sheet. Then save.

APPENDIX H
Standards and checking

STANDARDS AND CHECKLISTS

ACCURATE
- ☐ No circular references unless planned for
- ☐ Status bar does not say Calculate unless you fully intend it to
- ☐ No Excel error messages like **#REF!** or **#VALUE!**
- ☐ Accounts look reasonable. Scan from left to right across each account. Do any accounts rise or fall sharply in the first projected year? There may be an error somewhere
- ☐ Proofreading has been performed with satisfactory results:
  All formulas are accurate
  Formulas have been copied accurately
  Formulas refer to the right time period

FLEXIBLE
- ☐ No hard numbers in input formulas!
- ☐ In projections, formulas are copyable to all time periods
- ☐ If you change assumptions, the appropriate formulas change appropriately
- ☐ No more than one assumption per account, in one location

USER-FRIENDLY
- ☐ Complex calculations are split into simple steps
- ☐ Cover sheet contains relevant information about the mode
- ☐ Saved with cursor "homed" at the top of each sheet and the introductory sheet showing
- ☐ Numbers formatted with business formatting
- ☐ No numbers in italics
- ☐ Printed pages each have a header or footer showing date, name, name of model, and page number

Special checklist for projections
- ☐ Cash flow statement foots with balance sheet
- ☐ Balance sheet balances
- ☐ One assumption for each account and each time period (there may be exceptions, but not many)

PROOFREADING

You *have* to do it......No one wants to proofread, but if your career and your reputation rest on your model, you'd better do it. Almost no one can construct a complex model without making mistakes, either dumb and obvious or subtle.

Proofread on paper......You will catch errors looking at a paper copy that you'll never see on the screen.

CHECKING AND STANDARDS — APPENDIX H

Trace errors . . . . Trace errors with the double-click method (see Problem Set 1) and with auditing tools (**Tools Audi**t. Experiment with **Trace Precedents** and **Trace Dependents**.)

ERRORS
A list of the most common errors you will find on your models.

Circular reasoning errors

What are circular errors? . . . . Circular errors occur when a formula refers to itself, directly or indirectly.

The classic example of a CIRCULAR error:

	D
12	10
13	5
14	=SUM(D12:D14)

A formula with a circular reference

In the example, the formula is adding itself back into the sum. Excel tries to calculate what the answer should be but gives up and puts a zero in the cell.

	D
12	10
13	5
14	0	=SUM(D12:D14)

The result of the circular reference

In the example, the formula is adding itself back into the sum. Excel tries to calculate what the answer should be but gives up and puts a zero in the cell.

How you know you have one . . . . Excel warns you if you create a circular reference in a formula. It will not proceed unless you confirm that you want to go on.

The notice appears everywhere — Notice that when you have a circular reference, you can see a Circular notice on the Status bar. The notice appears on every open spreadsheet even if the circular reference is in another spreadsheet.

Another way to know — If you have formulas that show zeros when you know they should show a different result, you may have a circular reference.

Good or bad? . . . . Circular references are unacceptable unless you are deliberately using them to solve problems that cannot be solved any other way.

Say NO to iterations, unless... . . . . And if you have heard something about using iterations to "cure" circularities, don't! Not unless you understand iterations completely, know what the use of iterations does to your spreadsheet and how to fix the horrible problems that its use can generate.

194 Training for Finance

Excel error messages

#VALUE! . . . . Occurs in formula cells. You referred to a cell that does not contain a number. Excel is saying, "Get me a value!"

	C
7	8 percent
8	40
9	#VALUE!

=C7 * C8

Formula that refers to a label

In the example, **8 percent** is a label, not a value. Excel can't cope. Change the label to a number and the formula will correct itself.

#NAME? . . . . Occurs in formula cells. You used a word in the formula. Excel doesn't recognize the word as a range name and is asking for help. "Is this a range name?"

	C
7	8%
8	40
9	#NAME?

=C7 * percentage

Formula using an unrecognized word

#REF! . . . . The worst mistake of all. Excel has lost its cell reference in a formula. You can't recover — you have to rebuild the formula.

#REF! errors happen when cells are deleted (not cleared or erased, but actually deleted). If a formula referred to the deleted cell, the formula has been ruined.

	B
7	10
8	2
9	3
10	9

=B7 + B8 - B9

Good formula

	B
7	10
8	3
9	#REF!

=B7 + #REF! - B

Formula after B8 was deleted. Compare to good formula

ANSWERS　　　　　　　　　　　　　　　　　　　　　　　PART 1

Exercise 1: What are the cell addresses?　　　　　　　Page 9

	A	B	C
1			
2	A2		
3			C3
4	A4		
5		B5	
6			
7			
8			

Exercise 2: Lock your data up in cells　　　　　　　Page 19

1. Look at the example below. Which cell is the active cell (the cell the pointer is on)?

   B2 ▼ | 500

	A	B	C
1	Profit and	Year 1	
2	Sales	500	
3	Expenses	325	

   Cell address of the pointer: **B2**

2. Is the active cell being edited?

   ☐ Yes　　☒ No

3. How can you tell?

   The Edit bar doesn't show the red X and green check mark.

Exercise 3: Set up a small spreadsheet　　　　　　　Page 20

	A	B	C
1	Mfg. Expenses	Qtr 1	Qtr 2
2	Labor	8000	8025
3	Supplies	6000	6500
4	Electricity	200	240
5	Tool and die	750	750
6	Robotics	1000	1050
7	Depreciation	500	500

Before editing

	A	B	C
1	Manufacturing expenses	Qtr 1	Qtr 2
2	Labor costs	8125	8025
3	Materials	6000	6500
4	Electricity	200	240
5	Tool and die	750	750
6	Robotics	1000	1050
7	Depreciation	500	500

After editing

© 1998 Adkins & Matchett

ANSWERS — PART 1

Test #1 — Page 21

1. Yes, because you can see the X and the checkmark.
2. Use the Delete key. The other methods are either inefficient (Backspace) or wrong (spacebar).
3. Ready means no cell is being edited and you are free to start entering or editing.
4. False. If you widen a column, you widen all of it.
5. You should widen the column.

Exercise 4: Getting around the menus — Page 27

1. Which key do you press to get to the menu bar?

   > ALT

2. The Edit menu has a command called Clear. What can it erase?

   > All, Formats, Contents, Comments *(Excel 97)* / Notes *(earlier versions of Excel)*

3. How do you "throw away" an entry before you enter it?

   > Escape key

4. Which menu has commands that change the size of your view?

   > The **View** menu

5. Which menu has a command to delete a worksheet?

   > The **Edit** menu

Test #2 — Page 28

1. Excel does **not** automatically save your changes when you close a file.
2. To save an extra copy: File Save As
3. Close the file without saving it. Then reopen it.
4. You can't use the **Unhide Window** command unless you've already hidden a window.
5. The command is grayed out.
6. No. Don't type the .XLS extension.
7. ALT puts you on the menu bar. ESC backs you out of a menu.

---

198 Training for Finance

ANSWERS   PART 1

Exercise 5: Formula logic   Page 32

Three of these formulas won't work in Excel. Find them and describe what's wrong with them.

1. =(4+3)(5-2)   X   No multiplication sign

2. =4+3   OK

3. =12^2   OK

4. 15/3   X   No equal sign

5. =7(3-1)   X   No multiplication sign

Exercise 6: Write formulas   Page 33

A. Write formulas to fill in the large boxed cells. Use cell references!

	A	B	
1	Sales	400	
2	COGS as % of Sales	75%	
3	COGS	=B1 * B2	Sales * COGS as % of sales
4			
5	Cash	23	
6	Accounts receivable	42	
7	Inventory	12	
8	Total current assets	=B5 + B6 + B7	Add
9			
10	Net income	64	
11	Number of shares	150	
12	Earnings per share	=B10 / B11	Divide No. of shares into Net income
13			
14	Fixed assets	250	
15	Depreciation	140	
16	Net fixed assets	=B14 - B15	Subtract Depn from Fixed assets

continued on next page

© 1998 Adkins & Matchett   **199**

ANSWERS PART 1

B. Look at the numbers below. Use their cell addresses to write the following formulas:

HINT: Pay attention to order of operations! Use parentheses if necessary.

	A	B	C	D
1				
2		14		
3	2			
4				6
5	3			
6			11	
7				
8		4		

a. =(B2 – A3)^C6   Raise 14 – 2 to the 11th power.

b. =(A5 – A3)*B8   Subtract 2 from 3 and multiply by 4.

c. =A5 * B8 * D4 / A3   Multiply 3 times 4 times 6 and divide the result by 2.

d. =D4 + (A5 * C6)   Add 6 to 3 times 11.

Exercise 7. Build spreadsheets   Page 39

1. Find total property, plant and equipment (PP&E) costs:

	A	B
1	Plant, property and equipment	
2	Land	14000
3	Buildings	98000
4	Equipment	147000
5	Total PP&E	259000

=B2 + B3 + B4

What - If
What is Total PP&E if Land is 17500 and Equipment is 194600:

	A	B
1	Plant, property and equipment	
2	Land	17500
3	Buildings	98000
4	Equipment	194600
5	Total PP&E	310100

=B2 + B3 + B4

ANSWERS **PART 1**

2. Find retained earnings:

	A	B	
1	Retained earnings calculaton		
2	Last year's retained earnings	4010	
3	This year's net income	880	
4	Dividend payout	220	
5	This year's retained earnings	4670	=B2 + B3 - B4

What - If
What if dividends are raised to 300?

	A	B	
1	Retained earnings calculaton		
2	Last year's retained earnings	4010	
3	This year's net income	880	
4	Dividend payout	300	
5	This year's retained earnings	4590	=B2 + B3 - B4

3. Find cost of goods sold (COGS):

	A	B	
1	Sales	400	
2	COGS % of sales	70%	
3	COGS	280	=B1 * B2

What - If
COGS is 65% of sales

	A	B	
1	Sales	400	
2	COGS % of sales	65%	
3	COGS	260	=B1 * B2

Exercise 8.   SUM workout   Page 42

1.   Use SUM to add the subtotals:

	A	B	C	
1	Assets	Last year	This year	
2				
3	Cash	350	370	
4	Accounts receivable	840	790	
5	Inventory	475	490	
6	Total current assets	1665	1650	=SUM(C3:C5)
7				
8	Net PP&E	1440	1470	
9	Intangibles	900	705	
10	Other	140	155	
11	Total non-current assets	2480	2330	=SUM(C8:C10)
12				
13	Total assets	4145	3980	=C6 + C11

2.   What will *Total assets* be this year if ...
     This year's cash is **400** AND this year's inventory is **480** AND this year's intangibles are **1044**?

   | 4339 |

© 1998 Adkins & Matchett **201**

ANSWERS PART 1

Exercise 9   Formula and SUM function review   Page 44

	A	B	
1	Budget		
2			
3	Inflation index	5%	
4	Benefits as % of salaries	40%	
5			
6	Salaries	4670	
7	Benefits	1868	=B6 * B4
8	Overhead	1120	
9	Supplies	675	
10	Travel & entertainment	2355	
11	Budget	10688	=SUM(B6:B10)
12			
13	Inflation amount	534.4	=B11 * B3
14	Adjusted budget	11222.4	=B11 + B12

What-If No. 1

11008.64   What will the adjusted budget be if inflation is actually 3%?

What-If No. 2

11467.58   What will the adjusted budget be if inflation is 5% and benefits are 45% of salary?

Test #3   Formulas   Page 45

1. Which of the following shows a range?
   ☐ B3, C16   ☑ D44:E52   ☐ AZ242+BA361

2. You should always use cell references in formulas so that …
   ☐ You can play "What-if" games later
   ☐ Key numbers like a 5% inflation rate are visible on the spreadsheet instead of being buried in a formula
   ☑ Both of the above

3. You can indent subtotal labels by using spaces

4. Which of these formulas won't work, and why?
   a. =B4(C11+D14) **won't** work because it lacks the * multiplication sign.
   b. =D8+D9-C12+ **won't** work because it ends with an operation sign.
   c. =SUM(C14:D19) is fine.

5. Cells used in a formula cannot be empty.
   ☐ True   ☑ False

continued on next page

202   Training for Finance

ANSWERS   **PART 1**

Test #3   Formulas, *continued*

6. Write formulas to go in the boxed cells below. You should be able to do this without using Excel.

	A	B
1	Budget	
2		
3	Salaries	3200
4	Benefits	1184
5	Overhead	900
6	Supplies	775
7	Budget	6059
8		
9	Benefits % of salary	=B4 / B3
10	Salary as % of total budget	=B3 / B7

Exercise 10   Copy formulas and SUM function review   Page 49

	A	B	C	D	E	F	
1	Sales performance						
2						Individual	
3		Qtr 1	Qtr 2	Qtr 3	Qtr 4	totals	
4	Ancona	460	340	380	370	**1550**	=SUM(B4:E4)
5	Baker	200	300	400	450	**1350**	=SUM(B5:E5)
6	Casey	375	325	500	450	**1650**	=SUM(B6:E6)
7	Daggett	500	600	500	650	**2250**	=SUM(B7:E7)
8	Quarterly totals	**1535**	**1565**	**1780**	**1920**		
		=SUM(B4:B7)	=SUM(C4:C7)	=SUM(D4:D7)	=SUM(E4:E7)		

What-If

| 2346 |

What will be Daggett's total sales if her sales in Qtr 2 are 629 instead of 600 and in the 4th quarter are 717 instead of 650?

Test #4   Your first projection   Page 50

6. Write formulas to go in the boxed cells below. You should be able to do this without using Excel.

	A	B	C	D	E	
1	Assumptions	Qtr 1	Qtr 2	Qtr 3	Qtr 4	
2	COGS % of sales	70%	65%	68%	65%	
3	Op. expenses % of sales	22%	24%	23%	24%	
4	Other expenses % of sales	4%	3%	4%	5%	
5						
6	Income statement					
7	Sales	600	650	590	680	
8	COGS	420	422.5	401.2	442	=E7*E2
9	Gross margin	180	227.5	188.8	238	=E7-E8
10						
11	Operating expenses	132	156	135.7	163.2	=E7*E3
12	Other expenses	24	19.5	23.6	34	=E7*E4
13	Total expenses	156	175.5	159.3	197.2	=SUM(E11:E12)
14						
15	Net income	24	52	29.5	40.8	=E9-E13

| 13.6 |

Net income in 4th qtr if 4th qtr COGS is 68% and Op. expenses is 25%.

© 1998 Adkins & Matchett   **203**

Exercise 11   MOVE it!   Page 52

1. – 5. The completed exercise with formulas for the 4th quarter.

	A	B	C	D	E	
1	Assumptions	Qtr 1	Qtr 2	Qtr 3	Qtr 4	
2	COGS % of sales	70.0%	65.0%	68.0%	65.0%	
3	Op. expenses % of sales	22.0%	24.0%	23.0%	24.0%	
4	Other expenses % of sales	4.0%	3.0%	4.0%	5.0%	
5						
6	Income statement					
7	Sales	600.0	650.0	590.0	680.0	
8	COGS	420.0	422.5	401.2	442.0	=E7 * E2
9	Gross margin	180.0	227.5	188.8	238.0	=E7 - E8
10						
11	Operating expenses	132.0	156.0	135.7	163.2	=E7 * E3
12	Other expenses	24.0	19.5	23.6	34.0	=E7 * E4
13	Total expenses	156.0	175.5	159.3	197.2	=SUM(E11:E12)
14						
15	Net income	24.0	52.0	29.5	40.8	=E9 - E13

6. Move E8 to cell F8. Notice that the formula for Gross margin adjusts itself automatically.

	A	B	C	D	E	
1	Assumptions	Qtr 1	Qtr 2	Qtr 3	Qtr 4	
2	COGS % of sales	70.0%	65.0%	68.0%	65.0%	
3	Op. expenses % of sales	22.0%	24.0%	23.0%	24.0%	
4	Other expenses % of sales	4.0%	3.0%	4.0%	5.0%	
5						
6	Income statement					
7	Sales	600.0	650.0	590.0	680.0	
8	COGS	420.0	422.5	401.2		442.0
9	Gross margin	180.0	227.5	188.8	238.0	=E7 - F8

Test #5   Copy, Move, Delete   Page 56

1. If you *copy* the formula in the box to **C5**, what will appear in **C5**?
   ☐ 150   ☒ 300

2. If you *move* the formula in the box to **C5**, what will appear in **C5**?
   ☒ 150   ☐ 300

3. What will appear in Cell **B5** if you delete Row **2**?
   ☒ #REF!   ☐ 50

4. What will the sum function read if you delete Row 3?
   ☐ #REF!   ☒ 500

5. The **#REF!** message means a cell reference within the formula has been lost.

6. **#REF!** messages are
   ☐ not too bad   ☒ very serious

ANSWERS — PART 1

Final Test — Pages 69 – 70

1. a. Billco

	A	B	
1	Billco's debt	$65,000	
2	Interest rate on debt	7.50%	
3	Annual interest	$4,875	=B1 * B2

    What if the interest rate is 9%?

	A	B	
1	Billco's debt	$65,000	
2	Interest rate on debt	9.00%	
3	Annual interest	$5,850	=B1 * B2

    b. Car sale price

	A	B	
1	Dealer cost	$19,500	
2	Markup on car	8.00%	
3	Amount of markup	$1,560	=B1 * B2
4	Final sale price	$21,060	=B1 + B3

    What if the dealer cost is $18,000 and the markup is 10%?

	A	B	
1	Dealer cost	$18,000	
2	Markup on car	10.00%	
3	Amount of markup	$1,800	=B1 * B2
4	Final sale price	$19,800	=B1 + B3

    c. CopyCopyCo

	A	B	
1	Sale price of copier	$4,995	
2	CopyCopyCo's cost	$3,475	
3	Difference	$1,520	=B1 - B2
4	Profit margin	30.4%	=B3 / B1

2. Gross sales

	A	B	C	D	E	
1		Calculator	Laptop	Desktop	TOTALS	
2	Price	$ 12.99	$ 2,499.95	$ 1,899.00		
3	Sales					
4	Week 1	460	65	34	559	=SUM(B4:D4)
5	Week 2	350	60	15	425	copy of E4
6	Week 3	420	55	40	515	copy of E4
7	Total sales	1230	180	89	1499	copy of E4
8		=SUM(B4:B6)	copy of B7	copy of B7		
9	Gross sales	$ 15,977.70	$ 449,991.00	$ 169,011.00	$ 634,979.70	
		=B2 * B7	=C2 * C7	=D2 * D7		

© 1998 Adkins & Matchett

ANSWERS — PART 1

3. Income statement

	A	B	C	D	
1		Year 1	Year 2	Year 3	
2	Assumptions				
3	COGS % of sales	62%	63%	64%	
4	SG&A % of sales	24%	24%	25%	
5	Taxes % of EBIT	37%	37%	37%	
6					
7	Income statement				
8	Sales	850.0	975.0	1,125.0	
9	COGS	527.0	614.3	720.0	=D8 * D3
10	Gross margin	323.0	360.8	405.0	=D8 - D9
11	SG&A	204.0	234.0	281.3	=D8 * D4
12	Earnings bef. int. and taxes (EBIT)	119.0	126.8	123.8	=D10 - D11
13	Taxes	44.0	46.9	45.8	=D12 *D5
14	Net income	75.0	79.9	78.0	=D12 - D13

What if Year 3 SG&A = 23% and Sales go up to 1,150?

	A	B	C	D	
1		Year 1	Year 2	Year 3	
2	Assumptions				
3	COGS % of sales	62%	63%	64%	
4	SG&A % of sales	24%	24%	23%	
5	Taxes % of EBIT	37%	37%	37%	
6					
7	Income statement				
8	Sales	850.0	975.0	1,150.0	
9	COGS	527.0	614.3	736.0	=D8 * D3
10	Gross margin	323.0	360.8	414.0	=D8 - D9
11	SG&A	204.0	234.0	264.5	=D8 * D4
12	Earnings bef. int. and taxes (EBIT)	119.0	126.8	149.5	=D10 - D11
13	Taxes	44.0	46.9	55.3	=D12 *D5
14	Net income	75.0	79.9	94.2	=D12 - D13

4. #### means you must widen the column to see the formatted number.

5. ☑ 4.3467   ☐ 4.0

6. ☐ =C4   ☑ =C4 – #REF!   ☐ Nothing: it will automatically adjust

7. ☐ show #REF!   ☑ automatically adjust itself   ☐ not change

8. ☑ is unchanged   ☐ changes to reflect its new position

9. ☐ True   ☑ False

10. ☑ =B4(B3+C12)   ☑ C4-C5   ☐ =D11^(1–B2)

206 Training for Finance

PART 2 GENERAL BUSINESS PROBLEMS

PROBLEM SET 1 — SIMPLE MODELS

Jet
Pages 77 – 82

	A	B	
1	Don's discount model		
2	*Assumptions*		
3	Standard price	10,500,000	
4	Discount percentage	7.5%	
5	Discount for purchase without fittings	600,000	
6	Estimated cost of fittings	460,000	
7			
8	*Final sale price*		
9	Amount of discount	787,500	=B3 * B4
10	Sale price with discount	9,712,500	=B3 - B9
11	Net savings on fittings	140,000	=B5 - B6
12	Final sale price	9,572,500	=B10 - B11

Robert's savings program, 1
Pages 83 – 84

Original assumptions

	A	B	
1	Robert's savings planner		
2	*Assumptions*		
3	Annual after-tax income	$34,500.00	
4	Percentage of after-tax income saved	5%	
5	Number of savings periods per year	52	
6			
7	*Savings*		
8	Income per period	$663.46	=B3 / B5
9	Amount saved per period	$33.17	=B8 * B4
10	Savings per year	$1,725.00	=B9 * B5

© 1998 Adkins & Matchett

ANSWERS — PART 2

What if Robert saves 8% per month?   Pages 83 – 84

	A	B	
1	Robert's savings planner		
2	Assumptions		
3	Annual after-tax income	$34,500.00	
4	Percentage of after-tax income saved	8%	
5	Number of savings periods per year	12	
6			
7	Savings		
8	Income per period	$2,875.00	=B3 / B5
9	Amount saved per period	$230.00	=B8 * B4
10	Savings per year	$2,760.00	=B9 * B5

Robert's savings program, 2   Page 85
Original assumptions

	A	B	C
1	Robert's expense budget		
2	Assumptions		
3	Salary per month	$2,875.00	
4	Fixed expenses per month	$2,050.00	
5	Variable expenses % of salary	20%	
6			
7	Monthly budget		
8	Income		
9	Salary	$2,875.00	=B3
10	Expenses		
11	Fixed expenses	$2,050.00	=B4
12	Variable expenses	$575.00	=B9 * B5
13	Total expenses	$2,625.00	=SUM(B11:B12)
14	Income available for savings	$250.00	=B9 - B13
15			
16	Total savings per month	$250.00	=B14
17	Percent of salary	8.7%	=B16 / B9

NOTE: Yes, this layout is overkill. You can get the result in half the space. This layout is appropriate for a model that must show all secondary steps in detail. If you did it in less space and can do the What-If problem by changing assumptions, your layout is fine.

Always think about what your client needs to see. When you must take someone else through your logic, a detailed presentation is appropriate.

What if Robert cuts his fixed expenses to $2000 and his incidental expenses to 18%?

| $357.50 | Total savings per month | 12.4% | Percent of salary |

208 Training for Finance

ANSWERS PART 2

PROBLEM SET 2　　　　　　　DATA ANALYSIS

Sales performance　　　　　　　　　　Pages 87 – 91

	A	B	C	D	E	
1	Sales performance					
2						
3	3rd quarter sales performance					
4	Salesperson	Total sales	Goal	Met goal?	Avg. sales/mo.	
5	Andrew	1125	1250	NO	375	=IF(B5>=C5,"YES","NO")
6	Bethany	1320	1250	YES	440	=AVERAGE(B13:D13)
7	Curtis	1230	1200	YES	410	
8	Dorothea	990	1000	NO	330	
9						
10	Quarterly performance data					
11	Quarterly	Jul	Aug	Sep		
12	Andrew	400	350	375		
13	Bethany	450	400	470		
14	Curtis	300	400	530		
15	Dorothea	210	370	410		

Inventory　　　　　　　　　　　　　　　　Page 90

Original assumptions

	A	B	C	D	
1	Inventory	Item 1	Item 2	Item 3	
2	Inventory, beginning of day	190	25	450	
3	Units sold	60	3	270	
4	Inventory, end of day	130	22	180	=D2-D3
5					
6	Restock level	80	20	200	
7	Restock alert			RESTOCK	=iF(D4<D6,"RESTOCK","")
8	Average no. of items sold	111			

NOTE　You could use **D4<=D6** if you wanted to restock when the stock exactly matched the restock level.

What if 8 of Item 2 are sold?

7	Restock alert		RESTOCK	RESTOCK	=IF(D4<D6,"RESTOCK","")
8	Average no. of items sold	113			

NOTE　The actual average changes to 112.6666667. Simply reduce the number of decimal places if you're still in General format. Remember, Excel actually calculates with the full value of the formula (112.6666667).

© 1998 Adkins & Matchett　**209**

Stock portfolio

Original assumptions

	A	B	C	D	
1	Stock portfolio				
2	*Individual stock performance*				
3		Stock 1	Stock 2	Stock 3	
4	No. shares	500	400	100	
5	Purchase price	$47.00	$64.00	$75.00	
6	Today's price	$41.00	$69.00	$72.00	
7	Decision	LOSS	GAIN	LOSS	=IF(D6>=D5,"GAIN ","LOSS ")
8					
9	*Portfolio value*				
10	Today's value	$20,500	$27,600	$7,200	=D4*D6
11	Total value of holdings	$55,300			=SUM(B10:D10)

NOTES
1. I didn't like the way GAIN and LOSS lined up in the cell, so I cheated and stuck a space after each word in the IF statement. Now they line up with the number format I chose.

2. The purchase price is important down to the penny and should be shown to 2 decimal places. The total value of the holdings can be rounded.

What if Stock 3's price today is $78.00?

Stock 3 now shows a GAIN.

| $7,800 | Today's value, Year 3 | $55,900 | Total value of holdings |

ANSWERS — PART 2

PROBLEM SET 3   DATE MATH

The depreciation schedule   Pages 95 – 99
Original assumptions

	A	B	C	D	E	F	G
1	1997 Depreciation						
2		1997					
3	Milling equipment	54,795	=C13*G13				
4	Trucks	18,283					
5	Plant	218,493					
6							
7	*Constants*						
8	Days in year	365					
9	FY end	30-Sep-97					
10							
11		Purchase	Purchase	Yearly	Days de-	Depn days	
12	*Data*	date	price	depn	preciated	/ year	Depn. %
13	Milling equipment	14-Mar-97	500,000	20%	200	55%	11%
14	New trucks	2-Jan-97	98,500	25%	271	74%	19%
15	Plant	15-Nov-96	2,500,000	10%	319	87%	9%
	Formulas for Milling equipment:				=$B$9-B13	=E13/$B$8	=F13*D13

What if the truck depreciation is 40% instead of 25%?

30%	Depn %		29,253	Truck depreciation

Stock checker   Page 100
Original assumptions

	A	B	C	D	
1	Stock checker				
2	*Inputs*				
3	Stock	PowerCo	RetailHut	BizMag	
4	Today's price/share	$44.50	$125.88	$64.25	
5	Today's date	May 7, 1998			
6	Days for S-T cap. gain	182			
7					
8	*Stock performance*				
9	Purch. price / share	$42.38	$125.50	$72.13	
10	Purchase date	12-Mar-94	5-May-98	22-Feb-95	
11	Days held	1,517	2	1,170	=$B$5-D10
12	Performance	**GAIN**	**GAIN**	**LOSS**	=IF(D4>=D9,"GAIN","LOSS")
13	Type of capital gain		**SHORT-TERM**		
14	Formula for Type of capital gain, D13		=IF(D11>=$B$6,"","SHORT-TERM")		

NOTE   The solution shows two different date formats, one for *Today's date* and another for *Purchase date*.

© 1998 Adkins & Matchett   **211**

ANSWERS   PART 2

What if PowerCo were bought on November 14, 1997, for $41.00 per share?

PowerCo now shows a short-term gain.

| 174 | Days held |

Investment returns   Pages 101 – 102

Original assumptions

	A	B	C	D
1	**Investment returns**			
2	**Constants and assumptions**			
3	Desired return	10.000%		
4	Today's date	May 7, 1998		
5		Zero coupon	Painting	Gold
6	Purchase date	Jan 1, 1997	Feb 1, 1996	Mar 1, 1997
7	Buy price	10,000	10,000	12,000
8	Today's value	10,500	14,000	12,100
9				
10	**Investment performance**			
11	Return	3.694%	16.031%	0.704%
12	Decision	Goal not met	Met goal	Goal not met
	Return formula for D11:		=(D8/D6)^(1/($B$4-D7)*365)-1	
	IF statement for D12:		=IF(D11>=$B$3,"Met goal","Goal not met")	

NOTE Want to flex your formatting muscles? See if you can create a custom date format that lines up the end of the date with numbers in Comma format and shows the month with three letters. See Appendix D for help. (Don't get bogged down in this – you could waste a lot of time unproductively.)

P.S. The answer's at the bottom of the page, upside down.

What if the gold had actually been bought on June 1, 1997?

Goal not met

| 0.895% | Return |

Custom date format: [mmm d, yyyy]

PROBLEM SET 4   GROWTH CALCULATIONS

Growth accounts

Pages 103 – 108

Original assumptions

	A	B	C	D	E	
1	**How accounts grow**					
2	figures in millions					
3						
4	*Assumptions*	Constants	Year 1	Year 2	Year 3	
5	Sales growth / year		5%	6%	8%	
6	Fixed asset growth $ / year		70	100	125	
7	Acquisitions growth in $	10				
8	Depreciation growth / year	5%				
9						
10	*Results*	Baseline year	Year 1	Year 2	Year 3	
11	Sales	1,100	1,155	1,224	1,322	=D11*(1+E5)
12	Fixed assets	1,400	1,470	1,570	1,695	=D12+E6
13	Acquisitions	500	510	520	530	=D13+$B$7
14	Depreciation	300	315	331	347	=D14*(1+$B$8)

NOTE   You could skip the empty rows and enlarge the rows at the beginnings of sections.

What-If

What if Acquisitions grow at $12 million per year and sales growth per year rises as follows?

	Year 1	Year 2	Year 3
Sales growth / year	8%	10%	11%

536	Year 3 Acquisitions
1,451	Year 3 Sales

ANSWERS — PART 2

Space requirements — Page 109

Original assumptions

	A	B	C	D	E
1	**Space requirements**				
2	*Assumptions*				
3		Base Year	Year 1	Year 2	Year 3
4	Sq ft per person	140			
5	Growth in personnel		30%	20%	20%
6					
7	*Results*				
8	Personnel	32	42	50	60	=D8*(1+E5)
9	Space requirements	4,480	5,824	6,989	8,387	=$B$4*E8

NOTE You could skip the empty rows and enlarge the rows at the beginnings of sections.

What-If

What if personnel growth is actually 50% 30% 10%?

| 69 | Year 3 personnel |
| 9,610 | Year 3 space requirements |

Maria's calculator sale — Page 110

Original assumptions

	A	B	C	D	F
1	**Maria's price calculator**				
2	*Inputs*	Calc 1	Calc 2	Calc 3	Averages
3	Cost	$0.99	$2.44	$14.25	$5.89
4	Markup percentage	500%	450%	300%	417%
5	Sale discount	25%			
6					
7	*Results*				
8	Regular price	$5.94	$13.42	$57.00	$25.45	=AVERAGE(B8:D8)
9	Sale price per item	$4.46	$10.07	$42.75	$19.09

Formula for regular price, D8:   =D3*(1+D4)

What-If

What if the sale discount is 30% and the markups go up as follows?

	Calc 1	Calc 2	Calc 3
Markup percentage	550%	500%	400%

| 483% | Average markup % |
| $49.88 | Sale price, Calc. 3 |

214 Training for Finance

PROBLEM SET 5 — PV AND FV

Emma and Robert
Pages 113 – 117

Original assumptions

	A	B	C	
1		Present value of car payments		
2		Assumptions		
3		Monthly payment	$500.00	
4		Interest rate/year	8.000%	
5		Life of loan in years	5	
6		No. of periods/year	12	
7		Present value		
8		Total amount paid	$30,000.00	=C3*C6*C5
9		PV of payments	$24,659.22	=PV(C4/C6,C5*C6,-C3)
10		Robert's savings planner		
11		Assumptions		
12		Weekly savings	$50.00	
13		Number of savings periods per year	52	
14		Number of years of savings	5	
15		Interest rate on savings	5.500%	
16		Savings program		
17		Total amount saved	$13,000.00	=C12*C13*C14
18		Future value of savings	$14,954.22	=FV(C15/C13,C13*C14,-C12)

What-If

How much would Emma's car cost (after the down payment) if her payments were $500 a month at 9.5% interest?

| $23,807.41 | PV of Emma's payments (cost of car) |

What if Robert saved $60 a week at an interest rate of 5.625%?

| $18,003.56 | Robert's total savings after 5 years, at weekly compounding |

ANSWERS PART 2

Compare three annuities   Page 118
Original assumptions

	A	B	C	D	E	
1		Compare three annuities				
2		Annuities	Annuity 1	Annuity 2	Annuity 3	
3		Initial cost	$10,000	$10,000	$10,000	
4		Discount rate	8.000%	8.000%	8.000%	
5		Life in years	5	3	6	
6		Payment	$2,700	$4,500	$2,250	
7		Actual amount received	$13,500	$13,500	$13,500	=E6*E5
8		PV of amount received	$10,780	$11,597	$10,401	=PV(E4,E5,-E6)

What-If

What if Annuity 1 paid you $3,375 each year for 4 years? Would it be worth more than the original Annuity 1 offer?

$11,178   New PV of Annuity 1

Yes, it's worth more.

Bullets and single payments   Pages 119 – 120
Original assumptions

	A	B	C	
1		Present value of a bullet payment		
2		Bullet payment	$5,000	
3		Discount rate	7.000%	
4		Years until payment is due	5	
5		PV of amount received	$3,565	=PV(C3,C4,0,-C2)
6		Future value of a single deposit		
7		Amount deposited today	$5,000	
8		Life in years	10	
9		Interest rate	5.500%	
10		Compounding periods/yr	12	
11		FV of deposit	$8,655	=FV(C9/C10,C8*C10,0,-C7)

What-If

What's your opinion of the deal if the discount rate is 7%? $3,565   New PV
The new deal is better.

What if the compounding is monthly rather than daily? $8,655   New FV

216 Training for Finance

SET 6 NPV AND IRR

Factory purchase
Pages 121 – 125

Original assumptions

	A	B	C	
1		Return on new factory		
2		figures in thousands		
3		Cash flows		
4		D.R.	12.000%	
5		Price	($5,000.00)	
6		Cash flow, Year 1	$1,500.00	
7		Cash flow, Year 2	$2,000.00	
8		Cash flow, Year 3	$3,000.00	
9		Return		
10		NPV	$5,069.01	=NPV(C4,C6:C8)
11		Net present value	$69.01	=C10+C5
12		IRR	12.71%	=IRR(C5:C8)

What-If

What if the discount rate is 14%?

| ($120.36) | Net present value |
| 12.71% | IRR |

What if the discount rate is 12% and the initial cost is $4,500?

| $569.01 | Net present value |
| 18.41% | IRR |

© 1998 Adkins & Matchett

Compare three investments

Page 126

Original assumptions

	A	B	C	D	E	F	G	H	I
1	Comparing NPV and IRR calculations								
2		figures in thousands							
3				Initial		Cash flows			
4	Data		D.R.	Price	Year 1	Year 2	Year 3	Year 4	Year 5
5		Oil fields	9.50%	(1,000.0)	250.0	250.0	250.0	300.0	300.0
6		Bond	9.00%	(1,000.0)	90.0	90.0	90.0	90.0	1,090.0
7		Real estate	8.50%	(1,000.0)	200.0	200.0	200.0	300.0	600.0
8									
9	Results		NPV calc.	Net PV	IRR				
10		Oil fields	1,026.5	26.5	10.48%				
11		Bond	1,000.0	(0.0)	9.00%				
12		Real estate	1,126.3	126.3	12.38%				
		Row 12:	=NPV(C7,E7:I7)	=C12+D7	=IRR(D7:I7)				

What-If

What if the oil field's cash flow changed?

	Year 1	Year 2	Year 3	Year 4	Year 5
Oil field	200	200	300	400	300

$46.74   Oil field's net adjusted present value

What if the real estate's discount rate were 9%?

$108.75   Real estate's net adjusted present value

ANSWERS — PART 2

RATE and PMT functions — Page 127

Original assumptions

	A	B	C
1		**More financial functions**	
2		**Find the payment amount**	
3		Cost of car	$38,000
4		Down payment	0
5		Amount financed	$38,000 =C3-C4
6		Years of loan life	5
7		Time units per year	12
8		Interest rate	8.00%
9		Payment	$770.50 =PMT(C8/C7,C6*C7,-C5)
10			
11		**Find the interest rate**	
12		Loan amount	$4,495
13		Life in years	5
14		Payments/year	12
15		Monthly payments	$92.00
16		Monthly interest rate	0.70% =RATE(C13*C14,-C15,C12)
17		Annual interest rate	8.40% =C16 * C14

NOTE   Payment amounts are usually formatted in dollars and cents. You can choose to format the other money inputs in the same style if you prefer.

What-If

What is the car payment if you pay a down payment of $7,200?

| $624.51 |

Car payment per month with down payment applied

What is the **annual** loan interest rate if the monthly payments are $95?

| 9.77% |

Loan interest rate

© 1998 Adkins & Matchett

ANSWERS — PART 2

PROBLEM SET 7 — PROJECTION PREP

PP&E analysis
Pages 131 – 134

Original assumptions

	A	B	C	D	E	F
1		Plant, property and equipment (PP&E)				
2		figures in millions	Historical	\multicolumn{3}{c}{Projected}
3			Year 0	Year 1	Year 2	Year 3
4		**Assumptions**				
5		Growth in new purchases		5%	10%	10%
6		Sales of equipment % of new purch		5%	5%	5%
7						
8		**Projection**				
9		Gross fixed assets, beginning		4,000.0	4,299.3	4,628.4	=E12
10		New purchases	300.0	315.0	346.5	381.2	=E10 * (1 + F5)
11		Sales of old equipment	12.0	15.8	17.3	19.1	=F10 * F6
12		Gross fixed assets, ending	4,000.0	4,299.3	4,628.4	4,990.5	=F9+F10-F11

What-If

What if Growth in new purchases falls to 6% in Years 2 and 3, and Sales of equipment rises to 10% in Year 3?

| 353.9 | New purchases, Year 3 |
| $4,935.0 | Gross fixed assets, ending balance Year 3 |

ANSWERS PART 2

Retained earnings Page 135

Original assumptions

	A	B	C	D	E	F	
1		Retained earnings analysis					
2		figures in millions	Historical	Projected			
3			Year 0	Year 1	Year 2	Year 3	
4		*Assumptions*					
5		Net income		85.0	93.0	100.0	
6		Dividends % of net income		40%	40%	40%	
7							
8		*Projection*					
9		Retained earnings, beginning		500.0	551.0	606.8	=E12
10		Net income	80.0	85.0	93.0	100.0	=F5
11		Dividends	20.0	34.0	37.2	40.0	=F10 * F6
12		Retained earnings, ending	500.0	551.0	606.8	666.8	=F9 + F10 - F11

What-If

What if dividends were 40% of net income in all 3 projected years?

| 666.8 | Retained earnings at the end of Year 3 |

Growth accounts Pages 136 – 138

Original assumptions

	A	B	C	D	E	F	
		Plug account					
		figures in millions					
			Base Year	Year 1	Year 2	Year 3	
		Assets					
		Cash	65	75.0	70.0	65.0	=F11-SUM(F6:F7)
		Current assets	45	50.0	60.0	70.0	
		Fixed assets	150	200.0	250.0	300.0	
		Total assets	260	325.0	380.0	435.0	
		Liabilities and Equity					
		L&E	260	325.0	380.0	435.0	

The Balance Sheet must balance and there should be no circular references.

What-If

Current Assets are 85 in Year 3?

| 50 | Cash plug, Year 3 |

© 1998 Adkins & Matchett

SET 8 — PROJECTION ON ONE SHEET

The single-sheet projection, Income Statement and Balance Sheet

Pages 139 – 143

Original assumptions

	A	B	C	D	E
19			*Historical*		
20		**Income statement**	Year 0	Year 1	**Formulas for Year 1**
21		Sales	650.0	682.5	=C20*(1+D6)
22		COGS	400.0	423.2	=D20*D7
23		Gross margin	250.0	259.4	=D20-D21
24					
25		SG&A	169.0	177.5	=D20*D8
26		Net income before taxes	81.0	81.9	=D22-D24
27		Taxes	32.0	32.8	=D9*D25
28		Net income	49.0	49.1	=D25-D26
29					
30		**Balance sheet**			
31		*Assets*			
32		Cash	407.0	413.3	=D43-SUM(D32:D33)
33		Current assets	136.5	143.3	=D20*D11
34		Investments	353.0	395.4	=C33*(1+D12)
35		**Total assets**	896.5	952.0	=SUM(D31:D33)
36					
37		*Liabilities*			
38		Current liabilities	116.5	122.9	=D14*D20
39		Long-term debt	120.0	120.0	=D15
40		*Equity*			
41		Stock and APIC	420.0	420.0	=D17
42		Retained earnings	240.0	289.1	=D66
43		Total equity	660.0	709.1	=SUM(D40:D41)
44		**Total liabilities and equity**	896.5	952.0	=SUM(D37:D38,D42)

NOTES A good projection has copyable formulas in all the formula cells. If your Year 1 formulas are right, you will be able to copy them across and trust that all other years are right, too.

Single-sheet projection, Cash Flow and Calculations

Original assumptions

	B	C	D	
		Historical		
45	**Cash flow statement**	Year 0	Year 1	**Formulas for Year 1**
46	Net income		49.1	=D27
47	(Inc.)/dec. in operating assets		(6.8)	=C32-D32
48	Inc./(dec.) in op. liabilities		6.3	=D37-C37
49	Cash flow from operations		48.7	=SUM(D46:D48)
50				
51	(Inc.)/dec. in investments		(42.4)	=C33-D33
52	Cash flow from investing activities		(42.4)	=SUM(D51)
53				
54	Inc./(dec.) in debt		0.0	=D38-C38
55	Inc./(dec.) in capital stock		0.0	=D40-C40
56	Cash flow from financing activities		0.0	=SUM(D54:D55)
57				
58	Net change in cash		6.3	=SUM(D49,D52,D56)
59				
60	Balance Sheet change in cash		6.3	=D31-C31
61				
62	**Calculations**			
63	Retained earnings calculations			
64	Retained earnings at beg. of year		240.0	=C66
65	Net income	49.0	49.1	=D27
66	Retained earnings at end of year	240.0	289.1	=SUM(D64:D65)

What-If No. 1

The company wants to increase its profits. What will happen if it increases sales growth?

	Year 1	Year 2	Year 3
Sales growth	8.0%	12.0%	12.0%

Your results

| 63.4 | Net income, Year 3 |

- ☑ Yes ☐ No Does the balance sheet still balance?
- ☑ Yes ☐ No Does the cash flow statement still foot with the balance sheet?
- ☑ Yes ☐ No Do the different assumption changes produce changes in the accounts?
- ☑ Yes ☐ No Do the changes make sense? (If Sales goes up, does Net income go up?)

What-If No. 2

IMPORTANT! First change the sales growth assumptions back to their original values:

	Year 1	Year 2	Year 3
Sales growth	5.0%	6.0%	7.0%

ANSWERS
PART 2

What if the company cuts costs?

	Year 1	Year 2	Year 3
COGS	60.0%	60.0%	60.0%
SG&A	25.0%	25.0%	25.0%

Your results

| 69.7 | Net income, Year 3 |

- ☑ Yes ☐ No Does the balance sheet still balance?
- ☑ Yes ☐ No Does the cash flow statement still foot with the balance sheet?
- ☑ Yes ☐ No Do the different assumption changes produce changes in the accounts?
- ☑ Yes ☐ No Do the changes make sense? (If Sales goes up, does Net income go up?)

PROBLEM SET 9 — MULTIPLE SHEETS

Budget, *Assumptions* sheet Page 149 – 154

Original assumptions on *Assumptions* sheet

	A	B	C	D	E	F
1	Budget					
2			Base	Projected		
3	Assumptions		Year	Year 1	Year 2	Year 3
4	Inflation rate			3%	4%	5%
5	Benefits % of salaries			37%	37%	37%
6	Square feet of office space			2,200.0	2,200.0	2,200.0
7	Cost per square foot			120.0	120.0	120.0

NOTE Make sure you put Year 1 in the same column on both sheets! The same goes for the other years, too.

Budget, *Budget* sheet

Projection formulas

	A	B	C	D	Year 1 formulas
1	Budget				
2			Base		
3	Budget projection		Year	Year 1	
4		Salaries	360,000.0	370,800.0	=C4*(1+'Assumptions'!D4)
5		Benefits	133,200.0	137,196.0	=D4*'Assumptions'!D5
6		Cost of office space	264,000.0	264,000.0	='Assumptions'!D6*'Assumptions'!D7
7		Total	757,200.0	771,996.0	=SUM(D4:D6)

NOTES Now you can appreciate why entering formulas by typing them is not such a good idea.

As with the projection in Problem Set 8, your Year 1 formulas should be copyable. If Year 1 is right, the copies in other years should be right, too.

In "base case" projections, when you're looking at normal conditions, you may have some accounts that don't change, like the cost of office space and the square footage. Always make provision for them to change in later "What-If" scenarios.

What-If No. 1

What if the cost of office space rises to 135 per square foot in Years 2 and 3?

| 297,000.0 | Cost of office space, Year 3 |
| 851,731.6 | Total budget, Year 3 |

What-If No. 2

IMPORTANT! Change back to the original assumptions: 120 per square foot in all years

What if Benefits rise to 40% of Salaries in Year 3?

| 264,000.0 | Cost of office space, Year 3 |
| 830,879.0 | Total budget, Year 3 |

Oil field analysis

Page 155 – 156

Original assumptions and key results on *Summary* sheet

	A	B	C	D	E	F	G	H
1	Oilco oil fields		figures in thousands except where indicated by 2 decimal places					
2	Assumptions		Totals and Constants	Year 1	Year 2	Year 3	Year 4	Year 5
3	Oil sale price/barrel ($)			$11.00	$11.00	$11.00	$11.00	$11.00
4	Cost of land		125,000.0					
5	Extractable barrels		25,000.0					
6	% extracted		100%	10%	20%	30%	25%	15%
7	Costs % of revenues			40%	30%	25%	25%	25%
8								
9	Key results							
10	Cash flows		(125,000.0)	16,500.0	38,500.0	61,875.0	51,562.5	30,937.5
11	Internal rate of return		16.21%	=IRR(C10:H10)			Formula in G10:	
12	Total cash flows, Years 1-5		199,375.0	=SUM(D10:H10)			=Calcs!G6	

NOTE In a model like this, you may prefer to show key results right below the assumptions, as you see here.

Original calculations on *Calcs* sheet

	A	B	C	D	E	F	G	H
1	Oilco oil fields		figures in thousands except where indicated					
2	Calculations		Totals and Constants	Year 1	Year 2	Year 3	Year 4	Year 5
3	Barrels extracted		20,000.0	2,000.0	4,000.0	6,000.0	5,000.0	3,000.0
4	Revenues		220,000.0	22,000.0	44,000.0	66,000.0	55,000.0	33,000.0
5	Costs		60,500.0	8,800.0	13,200.0	16,500.0	13,750.0	8,250.0
6	Net profit		159,500.0	13,200.0	30,800.0	49,500.0	41,250.0	24,750.0

Barrels extracted: D3 =Summary!$C$5 * Summary!D6
Revenues : D4 =Summary!D3 * Calcs!D3
Costs: D5 =D4 * Summary!D7
Net profit: D6 =D4 - D5

What-If Scenario 1

What if the price of oil rises $1 a year after Year 1?

| 22.72% | IRR | 239,437.5 | Total cash flows, Years 1 – 5 |

What-If Scenario 2

IMPORTANT! Change back to your original assumptions for oil of $11.00 a barrel in Years 2 and 3.

What if the price of oil falls to $10 / barrel in Years 3, 4, and 5?

| 13.82% | IRR | 186,250.0 | Total cash flows, Years 1 – 5 |

Training for Finance

ANSWERS — PART 2

What-If Scenario 3

IMPORTANT! Change back to your original assumptions for oil of $11.00 a barrel in Years 2 and 3.

What happens if the number of extractable barrels is really 20,000,000? Assume this fact is discovered before drilling starts. Use the original oil price assumptions.

8.02%	IRR	159,500.0	Total cash flows, Years 1 – 5

SET 10 — MULTIPLE-SHEET PROJECTION

Project Copious Corp. for 3 years — Pages 157 – 161

Assumptions sheet

	A / B	C	D	E	F
1	**Copious Corp.**				
2	figures in thousands	*Hist*	*Proj*	*Proj*	*Proj*
3	**Assumptions**	Year 0	Year 1	Year 2	Year 3
4	*Income statement*				
5	Sales growth		8%	8%	10%
6	COGS % of sales		68%	68%	68%
7	Operating expenses % of sales		24%	24%	24%
8	Taxes % of Net inc. before taxes		40%	40%	40%
9	*Balance sheet*				
10	Asset assumptions				
11	Current assets % of sales		18%	18%	18%
12	Fixed asset growth		20%	20%	20%
13	Liabilities assumptions				
14	Current liabs. % of sales		15%	15%	15%
15	Long-term debt		250.0	300.0	350.0
16	Equity assumptions				
17	Capital stock		110.0	110.0	110.0

Calcs sheet

	A / B	C	D	E	F	
1	**Copious Corp.**					
2	figures in thousands	*Hist*	*Proj*	*Proj*	*Proj*	
3	**Calculations**	Year 0	Year 1	Year 2	Year 3	
4	*Retained earnings calculations*					
5	Ret. earnings at beg. of year		200.0	272.6	351.0	=E7
6	Net income		72.6	78.4	86.2	=IncState!F11
7	Ret. earnings at end of year	200.0	272.6	351.0	437.2	=SUM(F5:F6)

© 1998 Adkins & Matchett

ANSWERS　　　　PART 2

IncState sheet

	A	B	C	D	E	F	
1	Copious Corp.						
2		figures in thousands	**Hist**	**Proj**	**Proj**	**Proj**	
3	**Income statement**		**Year 0**	**Year 1**	**Year 2**	**Year 3**	
4		Revenues	1,400.0	1,512.0	1,633.0	1,796.3	=E4 *(1 + Assumptions!F5)
5		COGS	950.0	1,028.2	1,110.4	1,221.5	=F4 * Assumptions!F6
6		Gross margin	450.0	483.8	522.5	574.8	=F4 - F5
7							
8		Operating expenses	340.0	362.9	391.9	431.1	=F4 * Assumptions!F7
9		Net income before taxes	110.0	121.0	130.6	143.7	=F6 - F8
10		Taxes	44.0	48.4	52.3	57.5	=F9 * Assumptions!F8
11		Net income	66.0	72.6	78.4	86.2	=F9 - F10

BalSheet sheet

	A	B	C	D	E	F	
1	Copious Corp.						
2		figures in thousands	**Hist**	**Proj**	**Proj**	**Proj**	
3	**Balance sheet**		**Year 0**	**Year 1**	**Year 2**	**Year 3**	
4	Assets						
5		Cash	68.0	107.2	136.0	152.1	=F18 - SUM(F6:F7)
6		Current assets	252.0	272.2	293.9	323.3	=Assumptions!F11*IncState!F4
7		PP&E	400.0	480.0	576.0	691.2	=E7 * (1 + Assumptions!F12)
8		**Total assets**	**720.0**	**859.4**	**1,005.9**	**1,166.6**	=SUM(F5:F7)
9							
10	Liabilities						
11		Current liabilities	210.0	226.8	244.9	269.4	=Assumptions!F14 * IncState!F4
12		Long-term debt	200.0	250.0	300.0	350.0	=Assumptions!F15
13							
14	Equity						
15		Capital stock	110.0	110.0	110.0	110.0	=Assumptions!F17
16		Retained earnings	200.0	272.6	351.0	437.2	=Calcs!F7
17		Total equity	310.0	382.6	461.0	547.2	=SUM(F15:F16)
18		**Total L&E**	**720.0**	**859.4**	**1,005.9**	**1,166.6**	=SUM(F11:F12,F17)

NOTES　When you look at cross-sheet formulas on your own worksheet, you may notice that they appear with apostrophes around the sheet name: ='Assumptions'!F12. I have left those out of the answer formulas for easier reading.

Looking at these formulas, you can see why I recommend short sheet names. Cross-sheet formulas can get pretty long.

CFS sheet

	A	B	C	D	E	F	
1	Copious Corp.						
2		figures in thousands	Hist	Proj	Proj	Proj	
3	Cash flow statement		Year 0	Year 1	Year 2	Year 3	
4		Net income		72.6	78.4	86.2	=IncState!F11
5		(Inc.) / Dec. in current assets		(20.2)	(21.8)	(29.4)	=BalSheet!E6 - BalSheet!F6
6		Inc. / (Dec.) in current liabilities		16.8	18.1	24.5	=BalSheet!F11 - BalSheet!E11
7		Cash flow from operations		69.2	74.8	81.3	=SUM(F4:F6)
8							
9		(Inc.) / Dec. in PP&E		(80.0)	(96.0)	(115.2)	=BalSheet!E7 - Balsheet!F7
10		Cash flow from investments		(80.0)	(96.0)	(115.2)	=SUM(F9)
11							
12		Inc. / (Dec.) in total debt		50.0	50.0	50.0	=BalSheet!F12 - BalSheet!E12
13		Inc. / (Dec.) in capital stock		0.0	0.0	0.0	=BalSheet!F15 - BalSheet!E15
14		Cash flow from fin. activities		50.0	50.0	50.0	=SUM(F12:F13)
15							
16	**Net change in cash**			39.2	28.8	16.1	=SUM(F7,F10,F14)

NOTE   Notice that the Balance Sheet balances and the Cash Flow Statement foots with the Balance Sheet.

What-If Scenario 1

What if Copious increases its sales and taxes are reduced?

	Year 1	Year 2	Year 3
Sales growth / year	9.0%	10.0%	13.0%
Taxes % of Net inc bef. taxes	39%	38%	37%

95.6	Net income in Year 3
165.2	Cash, Year 3
453.3	Retained earnings, Year 3

ANSWERS　　　　　　　　　　　　　　　　　　　　　　　　PART 2

What-If Scenario 2

First, return to the original assumptions. What if Copious increases its assets?

	Year 1	**Year 2**	**Year 3**
Current assets	20.0%	20.0%	20.0%

86.2	Net income in Year 3
116.2	Cash, Year 3
437.2	Retained earnings, Year 3

In this scenario, *Cash* ☐ rose　　☑ fell　　☐ stayed the same.

What-If Scenario 3

First, return to the original assumptions. What if Copious increases liabilities?

	Year 1	**Year 2**	**Year 3**
Current liabilities	20.0%	20.0%	20.0%

86.2	Net income in Year 3
241.9	Cash, Year 3
437.2	Retained earnings, Year 3

In this scenario, *Cash* ☑ rose　　☐ fell　　☐ stayed the same.

NOTE　Understanding *why* the different accounts respond or don't respond to the changes requires a knowledge of financial accounting, which is beyond the scope of this book. For detailed info about how changes in different accounts drive bottom-line figures like Net income, see Adkins & Matchett's *Introduction to Accounting for Finance*.

INDEX

A

in cells, 63
#DIV/0, 80
#NAME?, 195
#REF! messages, 55, 80, 195
#VALUE!, 80, 195
A-B-C-D method of construction, 75
Absolute reference, 96, 97 - 98, 185 - 187
Alignment, 13, 64, 175
Amateur, 18, 107
Annuity, 118
Assumptions, 87, 132, 191
    growth, 104
Auditing tools, 194
Automatic number formatting, *See* Number formatting
AVERAGE function, 88, 169

B

B A S E analysis, 39, 132, 133, 135, 144
Balance sheet formulas, 143
Balance sheet, 136, 142
Beauty save, 192
Blank sheet, 171
Bold, 64, 175
Borders and patterns, 175
Bullet payment, 119
Business formatting, 98

C

Calculate message on Status Bar, 171
Calculations area, 144
Calculations, supporting or secondary, 143
Cash flow statement formulas, 145 - 146
Cash flow statement, 145
Cash plug, 144
Cell address, 8
Cell references in formulas, 32, 33
Cell width, 17
Cell, long entries in, 17 - 18
Charts, 68
Check mark on Edit Bar, 13
Check, Cash flow statement against Balance sheet, 146
Checking your model, 80, 81
Checking your model, checklist, 84
Checklists, 193
Circular reference, 85, 137, 171, 194 - 195
Clear Contents, 65
Clipboard, 47
Close a file, 25
Constant, 96, 104, 156, 191
Copy a sheet, 172
Copy command, 46 - 49
Copy formats, 176
Copy formulas, 48 - 49
COUNT function, 59
Cover sheet, 192
CTRL C, 46
CTRL X, 51
Currency and comma formats, 61
Custom format codes, 178
Custom format, 178
Cut command, 51 - 53

D

Dates, calculating with, 95 - 96
Decimal places, 62
Default toolbar settings, 174
Delete formats, 176
Delete rows / columns, 54 - 56, 181
Delete, with the Delete key, 14
Depreciation, 96
Dialog boxes, 24
Discount rate, 118, 122, 123
Discount, calculating a, 77 - 78
Drivers, 132

E

Edit a cell, 19
Edit Bar, 7, 15
Edit data, 18
Edit Paste Special, 110, 180
Efficiency, 164
Erase formats, 172, See also Formats, clear
Erase, with the spacebar, 16
Error messages, Excel, 80
Escape key, 10, 14
Excel troubleshooter, 171-172
Excel, different versions, 1
Exponentiation, 101

F

Figures in thousands or millions, 121
Formats, clear, 96
Formatting, automatic number, 176
Formatting, and calculation, 62
Formatting guidelines, 173
Formatting icons, 61
Formatting, and time wasting, 61
Formatting, text, 64
Formula checking with double-click, 107
Formulas and functions, common business, 167 - 170
Formulas appearing in cells, 172
Formulas in Excel, 31 - 40
Formulas, cell references in, 32, 33

INDEX

Formulas, consistent time units in, 113, 115
Formulas, cross-sheet, 153
Formulas, empty cells in, 40
Formulas, errors in, 43
Formulas, growth, 104, 106
Formulas, hard numbers in, 80 - 81, 98, 107
Formulas, negative growth, 110
Formulas, spaces in, 32
Freeze Panes, 142
Function key, F2, 18
Function, 114
Function, structure, 59
FV function, 116, 170

G

Graphs, See Charts
Grayed commands, 23
Gridlines, 188
Group and outline command, 187
Group Sheets, 150

H

Hard numbers, see Formulas
Headers and footers, 188, 189 - 190
Help, 58- 59
Hide rows / columns, 187
Historical information, 132

I

Icons, 58
IF function, 88, 90, 92, 114, 170
Income statement formulas, 141
Income statement, 141
Input data, 13
Inputs and outputs, 35, 77
Insert, columns, 54
Insert, rows, 54
Install Style icon, 179
Intermediate results, 78
IRR function, 123 - 124, 155, 170

Italics, 64
Iteration, 171, 195

K

Keyboard vs. mouse, 3, 23, 65
Keyboard, and stress, 3

L

Layouts, 191 - 192
Long entries, See Cell, long entries
Lotus, 1

M

MAX function, 169
Menu Bar, 7
Menus vs. icons, 22
Menus, submenus, 24
MIN function, 169
Model, using separate worksheets, 150
Models, 73
Multiple sheets, 66, 157, 192
Multiple sheets, delete or insert, 67
Multiple sheets, move, 67
Multiple sheets, naming, 67
Multiple sheets, print, 160
Multiple-sheet models, 150

N

Name Box, 7, 8
Navigate through sheets, 151
Navigation, 10 - 11,
Negative numbers, 16, 61
NPV function, 121, 122, 170
Num Lock key, 34
Number formats, 60, 173, 176 - 179
Number formats, automatic, 16
Number pad, 34, 172

O

Open a file, 26
Open a file, shortcut, 26
Operation signs, 31, 170
Order of operations, 31

P

Page break lines, 172
Page Break, 190
Paste, with Enter and with CTRL V, 51
Percent formats, 61
Plug accounts, 132, 136
PMT function, 127
Pointer, 7, 8
Portrait or Landscape, 189
Positive and negative numbers in projections, 134
Practice, the value of, 2, 4
Presentation, 58
Print Preview command, 188
Print selection, 160
Print Titles, 190
Print, 68, 188 - 190
Projection, 50, 131
Proofreading, 193
PV function, 115, 170

Q

Quattro Pro, 1

R

Range names, 183 - 185
Ranges, 40, 42, 46
RATE function, 127
Relative reference, 97, see also Absolute reference
Retained earnings, 143
Return on investment, 101

INDEX

S

Save a file, 24 - 25
Scientific format, 63
Sections within models, 139
Series Fill, 105, 182
Settings, 76
Shortcut, Open a file, 26
Shortcut, Undo/Redo, 29
Shortcuts, keyboard, 164 - 166
Shortcuts, mouse, 166
Single deposit, 119
Sort, 89
Standards, 193
Status Bar, 7, 15
Submenus, 24
SUM function and ranges, 42
SUM function shortcut, 41
SUM function, 168
SUM function, 41
SUM function, arguments, 59
SUM function, within another formula or function, 137

T

Text formats, 64, 173, 175
Toolbars, 7, 60, 172
Tools Options Edit, 107
Tools Options menu, 76
Totals and constants column, 156

U

Underscore, 64
Undo/Redo command shortcut, 29
Undo/Redo command, 29

V

View Zoom command, 187

W

What If?, 38, 74, 77, 81
What-If games, 147 - 148
Widen a column, 18
Wiggling box, 171
Window Arrange, 152
Window Split, 143, 152
Worksheets, multiple, 12
Wrap text, 106

© 1998 Adkins & Matchett